ABOUT THE AUTHORS

Sarah Edelman is a clinical psychologist, author and trainer. She has published many articles in professional and mainstream journals, and is author of the best-selling book on CBT, *Change Your Thinking*.

Louise Rémond is a clinical psychologist at the Health Psychology Unit, University of Technology, Sydney. She conducts psychological therapy and workshops with teenagers and adults, and for many years wrote the 'Dolly Doctor' Love and Life column for *DOLLY* magazine.

GOOD THINKING

A teenagers' guide to managing stress and emotions using CBT

Sarah Edelman PhD
and Louise Rémond M.Psych

ABC
Books

The ABC 'Wave' device is a trademark of the Australian Broadcasting Corporation and is used under licence by HarperCollins*Publishers* Australia.

First published in Australia in 2017
by ABC Books for the Australian Broadcasting Corporation
by HarperCollins*Publishers* Australia Pty Limited
ABN 36 009 913 517
www.harpercollins.com.au

HarperCollins*Publishers*
Level 13, 201 Elizabeth Street, Sydney NSW 2000, Australia
Unit D1, 63 Apollo Drive, Rosedale, Auckland 0632, New Zealand
A 53, Sector 57, Noida, UP, India
1 London Bridge Street, London SE1 9GF, United Kingdom
2 Bloor Street East, 20th floor, Toronto, Ontario M4W 1A8, Canada
195 Broadway, New York NY 10007, USA

National Library of Australia Cataloguing-in-Publication data:

Edelman, Sarah, author.
  Good thinking: a teenagers' guide to managing stress and emotions using CBT / Sarah Edelman, Louise Rémond.
  ISBN: 978 0 7333 3828 1 (paperback)
  ISBN: 978 1 4607 0821 7 (ebook)
  Notes: Includes index.
  Subjects: Behaviour therapy – teenagers.
  Cognitive therapy – teenagers.
  Self-help techniques.

Cover design by Hazel Lam, HarperCollins Design Studio
Cover image by shutterstock.com
Typeset in Adobe Caslon Pro by Kelli Lonergan
Printed and bound in Australia by McPhersons Printing Group
The papers used by HarperCollins in the manufacture of this book are a natural, recyclable product made from wood grown in sustainable plantation forests. The fibre source and manufacturing processes meet recognised international environmental standards, and carry certification.

Contents

This book is dedicated to all teenagers.

Happy reading and good thinking
Now and always.

Introduction

There's a lot going on when you're a teenager. Pressure is mounting from different directions: parents and teachers are telling you to be 'more responsible', friends are introducing you to all sorts of new ideas, and the media is constantly bombarding you with messages about how you should look and act if you want to be popular and successful. On top of that, exams are on the horizon and decisions will need to be made about your future.

There are also many changes to which you need to adjust: your body developing, shifts in the nature of your relationships and even adjustments in the way you think about things. You might find yourself questioning who you are and where you fit in. If you're like many teens, you might feel as though you're in limbo — you're definitely not a child any more, but you're not a fully fledged adult either. While the teenage years can be fun and exciting at times, they also bring many new challenges.

THE TEENAGE YEARS — WHAT'S HAPPENING?

When you're a teenager you are developing in different ways, including physically, emotionally and socially.

PHYSICAL CHANGES

The most noticeable changes that occur during adolescence are the physical ones. As a teenager, you have a body that is growing and developing into an adult. These changes may be obvious to others, as well as to you.

Puberty kicks off when chemical messengers in the brain trigger the release of sex hormones. These produce changes in height, weight and body shape. Your skin becomes oilier (often bringing those annoying pimples). Periods and breasts start developing for girls, while erections and breaking voices start happening for boys.

These changes may lead to feelings of self-consciousness. Many teenagers worry about how they look and what others think of them. Not everyone develops at the same pace, and some experience more noticeable changes than others. Provided you are healthy, (mostly) eating well, getting enough sleep and exercising, then your body will be at a stage that is right for you.

BRAIN CHANGES

Scientists used to think that our brains were almost fully developed by early childhood. We now know, however, that our brains go through an important stage of 'rewiring' from age twelve to our early twenties. As a result, many experts describe the teenage brain as 'being under construction'. The brain goes through a process of 'pruning', where frequently used connections are strengthened. For example, if you are practising an instrument, doing particular maths problems a lot or gaming for hours on end, these pathways in your brain will get stronger. Connections that are no longer relevant or used very much (like a language spoken for only the first few years of your life) gradually disappear.

While these brain changes are occurring, the way you think and the choices you make will also change. In younger teenagers, the emotional part of the brain plays a greater role in problem-solving and decision-making, which is why you may sometimes do 'not-so-sensible' things. You feel emotions more intensely, and may find yourself getting angry, anxious, sad or resentful more often than before. As you get older, other developments in your brain lead to changes in the way you think. For instance, you are better able to see other peoples' point of view, reflect on your own thinking and consider the future.

Like any new development, these changes take some getting used to, and can sometimes send you into 'overdrive'. For instance, many teens describe thinking about 'what if's' (that is, future possibilities and fears) and find themselves overthinking certain situations. You might find yourself thinking about deeper issues, such as love and spirituality, or becoming preoccupied with how others see you.

SOCIAL DEVELOPMENT AND A STRONGER SENSE OF IDENTITY

To move successfully from being a child to an adult, you need to become more independent. It is normal to want more freedom to do your own thing and make your own decisions. Your greater ability to think critically may cause you to challenge rules imposed on you by adults. This can be tough for parents and other adults who want to protect you, and may not think you are ready for the level of independence you are seeking. It can sometimes feel like a tug of war between you and them, which can lead to tensions and arguments on the home front.

The teen–adult struggle that often occurs is normal during adolescence. It is part of the transition from total dependence on your parents and family in childhood, to independence as an adult. Most teenagers want to separate from their parents, and move towards friends and peers as their inner circle with whom they can bounce ideas off and hang out. This transition takes some adjusting to — not just for you, but for others in your life as well.

Another part of adolescence is developing a stronger sense of your own identity. During the teenage years, it is normal to be asking yourself questions like: 'Who am I?' and 'Where do I fit in?' When you were younger, your identity was shaped by your family and early experiences. As a teenager, with your new thinking and all the other changes you are going through, this sense of identity is something you are beginning to explore more for yourself. This can be exciting, daunting and confusing all at the same time.

As part of your investigation into 'Who is the real me?' you will more than likely be questioning many different aspects of yourself and your world. These may include:

➤ friendships (e.g. 'Do I really belong in this group?'; 'Do I have anything in common with my old friends any more?')

➤ relationships and sexuality (e.g. 'Who am I attracted to?'; 'How do I act around someone I like as more than "just friends"?')

➤ interests (e.g. 'Do I still like the music I used to listen to?'; 'What do I feel passionate about?')

➤ personal style (e.g. 'How do I want to present myself to the world?'; 'How do I like to dress?')

➤ values and morals (e.g. 'What do I stand for?'; 'What is truly important to me?')

➤ the future (e.g. 'What are my goals?'; 'What kind of life do I want?')

➤ spirituality/religion (e.g. 'Do I believe in the religion I was raised with?'; 'Do I share my parents'/friends' beliefs?').

There are many dimensions to you as an individual that you may never have thought about much before. You don't need to find answers to these questions right away — our sense of identity unfolds over many years as we live our lives and make greater sense of ourselves and our world.

ABOUT THIS BOOK

Although our teenage years involve some particular challenges, the hard times do not suddenly stop the moment we become adults. At every stage of our lives, there are stressful events. There are also times of joy, excitement and contentment. If we can learn to manage challenging situations so that they don't create too much turmoil, we can enjoy happier, more fulfilling lives. We may not be able to prevent some stressful situations happening, but we can learn to respond to them in a way that minimises any negative fallout they have for us emotionally.

While we tend to assume that our life experiences determine the way we feel, in actual fact the most important thing is *the way we think about them*. Learning to think in a healthy and balanced way helps us to avoid a lot of unnecessary distress, and to bounce back more quickly when stressful events happen. It may also motivate us to problem-solve during challenging situations, and, therefore, be more in control.

Cognitive behavioural therapy (CBT) is a psychological skills-based approach to managing stressful life situations and upsetting emotions, by enabling you to challenge unhelpful thinking habits and see things in a more reasonable, balanced way. Hundreds of studies have shown that using techniques based on CBT can help people reduce their chances of becoming emotionally overwhelmed, and allows them to recover more quickly when they experience mental-health problems.

The word 'cognitive' refers to our thought processes, and includes both our *thoughts* and *beliefs*. The central idea of CBT is that usually when we feel bad, it is because of our cognitions. If we can change our thoughts and beliefs, we can change the way we feel, even when we can't change the situation.

The word 'behavioural' refers to actions we can take to change the way we think and feel. Typical behavioural strategies used in CBT include:

➤ Experimenting with new behaviours that we would normally avoid (such as inviting someone to catch up, speaking up in class, or joining the school band)

➤ Confronting our fears by repeatedly doing things that feel scary

➤ Exploring various solutions to our problems, choosing a strategy and putting it in place

➤ Communicating more effectively with others

➤ Deliberately doing things we enjoy, or that give us a sense of achievement to help lift our mood

➤ Practising relaxation and mindfulness techniques

The strategies described in this book are based on CBT, and will give you the tools to help you manage many of the challenges you are likely to face now and in the future. While unpleasant emotions like anger, anxiety, sadness and guilt are a normal part of being human, using CBT strategies can help you to bounce back from them more quickly and, sometimes, avoid them altogether. They can also make you more resilient when facing stressful life events, and enable you to feel better about yourself as a person.

Most importantly, learning these strategies at this stage will equip you with a set of skills that you can use throughout your adult life. Indeed, many adults who have learned to use CBT strategies have commented to us, 'I wish someone had taught me this at school. It would have made my life so much easier.' (Both authors of this book certainly wish we had learned to use CBT when we were teenagers.) Many experts argue that the earlier people learn these techniques, the greater their protection from mental-health problems later in their lives.

Finally, it is important to say that while this book will be a useful resource for managing emotions, it may not always be enough. If you are experiencing severe stress, or feeling overwhelmed by anxiety, hopelessness or any intense emotions, please talk to an adult that you trust. Opening up to family members, teachers, a school counsellor or supportive friends can make a big difference to the way you feel. We have also provided a list of useful resources in the back of this book if you feel like you need some additional support. However, if none of this seems to help, it is important to speak to your GP. They will ask you about what has been happening and may provide a referral to see a mental-health professional. Talking to someone with experience in treating mental-health problems can help you to see things differently, and to address the specific challenges you are dealing with. This will enable you to get back on track more quickly.

To all readers of this book, we wish you happy reading and good thinking, now and always!

Sarah and Louise

ONE

Thoughts, Feelings and Behaviours

Have you ever found yourself stressing about something for days and then a week later realised that it really didn't matter at all? Perhaps you talked it over with a friend or family member and felt much better afterwards? Although the situation hadn't changed, you started to think differently about it, and as a result your mood lifted. This experience illustrates an important principle in psychology:

> The way we think determines the way we feel.
> Changing how we think will change how we feel.

At times, things go wrong, people let us down, we make mistakes and disappointments happen. In the end, it is the way we think about those situations that determines how we feel about them. Sometimes we can make ourselves totally miserable, even when our situations are really not that bad, simply by thinking in a negative, self-defeating way.

Perhaps you have also noticed that people can react differently when they are in the same situation. Imagine two girls who are academically very similar (that is, both are equally bright and have spent about the same amount of time studying) going into their first Year 12 exam. One is completely frazzled, while the other is a bit nervous, but basically feeling OK. Why are their reactions so different? It's not the situation itself, but the way they are thinking about their situation that determines how they feel and behave. The girl who is stressed out about her exam is thinking: 'This is so bad... Everything is riding on this ... If I don't do well, everyone will think badly of me and I'll completely ruin my future.' Meanwhile, the other girl is thinking: 'Exams are always nerve-racking, but I've done them lots of times before and I know it's not so bad once I get started. I've been going OK up until now, so chances are it will be OK this time. I can only do my best.'

This example demonstrates how our thinking largely determines how we feel (from being totally stressed out to just a bit nervous). Our thoughts and beliefs also affect the way we *behave*.

Imagine two guys walking into a party where they don't know anyone. One starts talking to people within a few minutes of arriving, even though he feels a bit nervous; the other looks around for a corner to hide in.

In this example, the first guy believes he is likeable and finds it easy to be friendly, as he assumes that others will be friendly back to him. As a result, he is motivated to approach new people and start conversations (behaviour). In contrast, his friend has low self-esteem and expects others will react negatively towards him. He thinks to himself: 'I can't just go up and talk to strangers ... They'll probably ignore me and I'll look like a complete idiot.' Consequently, he keeps to himself (behaviour).

THOUGHTS

As we go about our daily lives, we are constantly thinking about and making sense of the situations in which we find ourselves. It is as though we have an internal voice inside our heads that is commentating on our experiences. This inner voice includes our thoughts (sometimes called 'self-talk'), as well as our deeper-level beliefs about ourselves and the world. Our self-talk is automatic and feels like 'fact' or 'truth', but actually it is just our interpretation and is not always correct. Much of our self-talk is reasonable (e.g. 'I'd better do some study for that exam'; 'I'm really looking forward to that game'; 'He seemed very quiet tonight'). However, some of our self-talk is negative, incorrect or self-defeating (e.g. 'I'm going to fail for sure'; 'I didn't play well — I'm so hopeless!'; 'He was quiet all night — it must be because he doesn't like me'). Negative self-talk often causes us to feel bad, and to experience upsetting emotions such as frustration, sadness, guilt, hurt, anger or anxiety.

Our thinking can be reasonable or unreasonable; it can contain a grain of truth or it can be wildly distorted. The thing to remember is that just because you think something, doesn't make it true.

JANA was waiting in a queue at the supermarket when she looked around and saw Sara, a girl from her class, walking towards her. Jana smiled at Sara, but Sara walked straight past her without acknowledging her.

What would you make of this situation if you were Jana? One interpretation might be that Sara was deliberately ignoring her. For example, Jana might think: 'What have I done wrong? I must have done something to upset her.' This self-talk would probably leave Jana feeling bad — worried that she'd done something to offend Sara, and guilty about upsetting her. Or Jana could think: 'How rude is she? What an absolute snob! All she needs to do is say "hello". I just can't believe that someone can act like that!' This interpretation would leave Jana feeling angry and determined to be rude to Sara the next time she sees her.

Let's 'take two', and imagine Jana knew that Sara wore glasses. How might this affect her self-talk about the situation? Jana might think: 'She makes me laugh — she never wears her glasses and she can't see a thing without them.' How would Jana be feeling if this was what she was thinking? Probably amused, and keen to call out to Sara.

Or Jana could also have thought, 'Sara seems totally caught up in her own little world — I wonder if something's happened? I know her mum has been quite sick.' If this had been her interpretation, Jana may feel concerned, and she may want to go up to Sara and ask if everything is all right. Alternatively, if she just thought, 'Sara obviously didn't see me,' she probably wouldn't think much about it.

So you can see that it is not only the things that happen that determine how we feel, but also the way that we interpret them.

EMOTIONS

Our emotions determine how we feel — whether we feel good or bad, or somewhere in between. Sometimes, we experience positive (pleasant) emotions such as excitement, satisfaction or enjoyment. At other times, we experience negative (unpleasant) emotions such as anxiety, sadness, frustration, hurt, resentment, anger or shame. Our emotions are largely influenced by our thoughts (perceptions), and are accompanied by physical (body) sensations. In fact, many unpleasant emotions feel bad because of the uncomfortable physical sensations they produce, such as tension in the chest and shoulders; churning stomach; revved-up, jittery sensations; heat surges and increased heart rate. If you were to close your eyes and tune in to what is happening in your body the next time you feel anxious, angry, frustrated or despondent, you would notice very specific sensations connected to those emotions.

Although most people don't like experiencing unpleasant emotions, these feelings can play a positive role in our lives. *Emotions motivate behaviours* and when they encourage us to do things that are in our own best interests, they serve us well (even if they are unpleasant). For example, anxiety before an approaching job interview or exam can motivate you to do some preparation; anger in response to poor service can motivate you to be more assertive than usual; and guilt in response to having said something hurtful to a friend might motivate you to call them and apologise.

While unpleasant emotions can motivate us to do things that help us get what we want, sometimes we ignore their messages. For example, have you ever found yourself feeling guilty about not studying, but not doing anything about it? Or feeling angry about something that you think is unfair, but not trying to resolve it? At other times, we might act in ways that actually make the situation worse. So, for example, if feeling ashamed stops you from going to school, or if feeling sad leads you to avoid people, or if feeling anxious causes you to procrastinate, or if feeling angry causes you to act badly towards a friend, those behaviours are *self-defeating*. Ultimately, they prevent you from getting the things you want in life.

BEHAVIOURS

The things we do (our behaviours) have a big influence on the quality of our lives. Our behaviours include things like going to school each day, hanging out with particular friends, talking to our parents or teachers, watching TV, eating chocolate cake, studying in the library, scrolling through social media, going for a run, spreading gossip, joining a club, going to sleep, sticking posters on the bedroom wall, and thousands of other things in between.

Our behaviours can be helpful or unhelpful. Helpful behaviours move us towards the things that we want and value in our lives, such as having friends, doing well at school, being healthy and having fun. Unhelpful behaviours move us away from the things we want and value. So, for instance, you might find yourself putting off homework assignments that need to be done, avoiding opportunities to connect with friends, lashing out in anger at a family member or eating lots of junk food.

Our behaviours are influenced by our perceptions — that is, our thoughts and beliefs. So, for instance, if you believe that you should always be punctual, you are more likely to plan ahead to arrive at places on time. If you believe that people are likely to reject you, you are more likely to try too hard to please others, and find it hard to say 'no'. If you believe that putting effort into pursuing your goals will lead to success, you are more likely to work hard in order to succeed. However, if you believe that everything you do must be perfect, this may cause you to put too much pressure on yourself. As a result, you may procrastinate or spend too long completing tasks.

IN A NUTSHELL ...

➤ Our thoughts and beliefs (perceptions) affect our emotions and therefore influence the way that we feel much of the time.

➤ Emotions play an important role in motivating our behaviours. Even unpleasant emotions, such as anxiety, anger, sadness and guilt, can be helpful when they motivate us to do things that are consistent with our goals.

➤ Our behaviour can have a significant effect on our quality of life and is strongly influenced by our thoughts and beliefs.

TWO

Our ABCs

In the 1970s, a psychologist called Dr Albert Ellis described the connection between our thoughts, emotions and behaviours by referring to the 'ABC' of our experiences.

A IS FOR 'ACTIVATING EVENT'

The 'Activating Event' is the situation or trigger that 'activates' your emotional response. It might be losing your phone, having too much homework and not enough time to complete it, or a critical comment made by a friend.

B IS FOR 'BELIEFS'

(Note that this category actually includes both our *thoughts and beliefs*, but we often refer to it as 'Beliefs', because that starts with a 'B'.) Our thoughts are the various ideas that pop into our minds thousands of times a day ('I hope I can get there on time … It's Joe's birthday on Sunday … I must remember to return that book … I wonder what's for dinner …'), while our beliefs are the more basic and unchanging assumptions that we hold about ourselves and the world. 'I'm not good enough', 'I am likeable', 'People should do the right thing', 'I should always be punctual' and 'If I am friendly to others, they will be friendly to me' are examples of beliefs. Many of our beliefs are unconscious (that is, we are not even aware of them).

C IS FOR 'CONSEQUENCES'

Our Bs (thoughts and beliefs) affect us in two ways: they influence our *emotions* and our *behaviours*. These are referred to as 'Consequences' (our Cs).

When something happens and we feel upset, we usually assume that 'A' (the Activating Event) has made us feel that way. However, it is actually 'B' (our Beliefs and thoughts) that makes us feel the way we do. So, for instance, when Corrine felt awkward when she was around a guy she liked, she blamed herself: 'Ewan must think I'm a loser. I couldn't say anything, or even look at him … How pathetic am I?' This line of thinking made her feel ashamed and worthless (Consequences — emotions). As a result, she avoided going to places where she might bump into Ewan (Consequences — behaviour).

When Richie recently failed a test, he thought to himself: 'I failed the test because I didn't study.' This made him feel disappointed, but not hopeless (Consequences — emotions), because Richie believes that he can do well if he tries. The disappointment motivated him to knuckle down and study for his next exam (Consequences — behaviour).

Have a look at Scott's, Cathy's and Tony's examples, which illustrate the ABC of their self-talk:

SCOTT

ACTIVATING EVENT	Got my exam timetable.
BELIEFS/THOUGHTS	I'm not going to be able to do this. I'll fail, and the whole thing will be a disaster. My parents will be disappointed in me. I won't get into the course I want and then I won't be able to get a proper job … I'll end up a loser.
CONSEQUENCES How did I feel? What did I do?	 Felt stressed, panicky, butterflies in the stomach. Couldn't bring myself to sit down and study. Sat in front of the TV and ate two packs of chips.

CATHY

ACTIVATING EVENT	Looking at myself in the mirror.
BELIEFS/THOUGHTS	I look absolutely disgusting — I am so ugly. No wonder I don't have a boyfriend. Who would want a girlfriend who looks like this? My skin looks awful and my hair is terrible … Everyone will notice how bad I look. Why can't I just look like Rachel? She's perfect …
CONSEQUENCES How did I feel? What did I do?	Depressed, hopeless. Stayed home instead of going out with friends.

TONY:

ACTIVATING EVENT	Missed what could have been the winning catch at school cricket match.
BELIEFS/THOUGHTS	I can't believe what an uncoordinated idiot I am! That was a straightforward catch. How did I miss it? I shouldn't be playing on the team. I've let everyone down.
CONSEQUENCES How did I feel? What did I do?	Frustrated, embarrassed, ashamed, miserable. Just left straight after the match and went home. Decided not to go to the end-of-season cricket dinner.

OVER TO YOU …

The best way to make sense of the connection between A (Activating Event), B (Beliefs and thoughts) and C (Consequences) is to see how it applies to our own experiences. Why not have a go?

Think of a situation where you found yourself feeling bad in the last two weeks. For example, you may have been feeling upset, stressed, angry, sad, anxious, embarrassed or guilty.

In the Stress Log below, briefly describe the situation next to 'Activating Event'. Then, next to 'Beliefs' and 'Thoughts', write down the thoughts that were going through your mind at the time (we will look more closely at

Beliefs in Chapters 3 and 4). Finally, next to 'Consequences', write down how you were feeling and what you did.

Hint: when you describe the Activating Event, be sure to stick to facts. For example: 'I tried on my jeans and they were too small', NOT 'I tried on my jeans and I looked fat and disgusting!'; or 'Ewan said "hi" to me and I blushed and looked away', NOT 'Ewan said "hi" to me and I made a total fool of myself'.

STRESS LOG

ACTIVATING EVENT

BELIEFS/THOUGHTS

CONSEQUENCES
How did I feel?

What did I do?

Now think of another situation where you felt bad, and fill in your A, B and C on the form below.

STRESS LOG

ACTIVATING EVENT

BELIEFS/THOUGHTS

CONSEQUENCES
How did I feel?

What did I do?

One of the most helpful skills for developing good thinking is to notice any negative or self-defeating thoughts that pop into your mind. Learning to recognise faulty or unreasonable thinking will direct your attention to self-talk that you can challenge or change. In future chapters, we will look at how you can do this.

IN A NUTSHELL ...

➤ Our emotional responses are usually triggered by an Activating Event. Our Beliefs and thoughts determine the Consequences (our emotions and behaviours). This can be described as the ABCs of our experiences.

➤ Using a Stress Log to monitor our As, Bs and Cs can help us to notice instances of unhelpful thinking, and better understand the way that our thoughts and beliefs affect our emotions and behaviours.

THREE

Common Thinking Errors

When it comes to negative thinking, there are some common traps into which people fall. We call these 'thinking errors', because they are not an accurate or reasonable way of perceiving our situations. Thinking errors are a major cause of upsetting emotions and self-defeating behaviours. Whenever you find yourself feeling upset (e.g. anxious, angry, depressed, resentful, guilty or ashamed), it is helpful to look out for any thinking errors you might be making. Some of the most common ones are described below. Which of these apply to you? Remember, most of us slip into these unhelpful patterns at least some of the time.

Here are ten common thinking errors and ways to challenge them.

1. BLACK-AND-WHITE THINKING

You see everything in terms of good or bad, with no in-betweens. Either you've done a brilliant job, or you completely 'bombed'. If you're not a model lookalike, then you must be ugly. If you do something wrong, then you are a complete idiot. Your parents or teachers are either amazing or awful.

Examples

> ZORAN'S *band played their first gig at the local 'Battle of the Bands'. While some of the people in the crowd were paying attention*

and getting into the music, others were talking and not focused on their performance. Zoran left feeling low. He thought to himself, 'That was a disaster! No one was listening.' The reality was that some people were interested and others weren't, but the band played quite well and received some positive feedback.

TERRY'S performance on the debating team was not up to his usual high standards. Although he was still pretty good, Terry feels despondent because he tells himself that he was hopeless.

THE CHALLENGE: Avoid black-and-white thinking.

Look out for extremes. Most things are not black or white — usually they are somewhere in between. Just because something is not perfect, that doesn't mean that it's a complete write-off.

Ask yourself

> ➤ Is it really so bad, or am I seeing things in black and white?
> ➤ What's a more balanced way to think about this situation?

Reflect

Can you think of a time when your thinking was black and white? Describe it here:

2. COMPARING

We sometimes make comparisons between ourselves and other people, particularly those who we see as having a specific advantage in some area. Making comparisons is biased, because we are contrasting ourselves only with people who we think are 'better off' than us in some way, and leaves us feeling like we aren't good enough.

Examples

> *Whenever LEAH flicks through her favourite magazine, she thinks to herself, 'That model is so perfect … My legs are fat and stumpy compared to hers … Look how flat her tummy is — mine's just flab.' Whenever Leah goes to a party with her boyfriend, she spends most of the night comparing herself with the girls who she thinks are particularly beautiful, and ends up feeling inadequate.*

> *CRAIG's older brother Steven was a gifted student and came top of the school with his Year 12 results. Craig feels inadequate because he constantly compares himself to Steven. Although Craig is doing well on his assignments, he is unable to achieve Steven's brilliant results.*

THE CHALLENGE: Stop comparing.

Ask yourself
- ➤ Am I comparing myself with others?
- ➤ Is it a fair comparison? Is it helping me in any way?

Reflect
Can you think of a time when you were comparing? Describe it here:

3. FILTERING

When we filter, we do two things: first, we home in on the negative aspects of a situation, and second, we ignore or dismiss all the positive aspects.

Examples

> *As part of his English project, RICKY gave a presentation and his classmates were asked to provide written feedback. Most comments were positive, but two were critical. Ricky keeps focusing on the two critical comments, but ignores the twenty-five other comments that were positive.*

CASSIE has been feeling depressed and finds herself thinking back to negative things that happened earlier in her life. She keeps remembering times when she felt left out or rejected; however, she ignores the many positive experiences that she has had since then.

THE CHALLENGE: Consider the whole picture.

Ask yourself

➤ Am I just looking at the negatives, while overlooking the positives?

➤ What positive things am I ignoring?

Reflect

Can you think of a time when you were homing in on negative information and ignoring all the positive information (that is, filtering)? Describe it here:

4. PERSONALISING

When we personalise, we take things personally, even when the situation is not about us. We might take responsibility for things that go wrong, or we might feel accountable for other people's feelings, when it's not our fault.

Examples

Nicky told her boyfriend, VINCE, that she will not be able to go out during the week over the next four months, as she needs to focus on preparing for her Year 12 exams. Vince feels devastated. His immediate thoughts are: 'She's bored with me … She's trying to give me the flick.'

GORDON's friend Sam has been quiet all night, and Gordon assumes that Sam must be upset about something that he has said or done. In fact, Sam is feeling down because he just found out that his family will be moving interstate again at the end of the term, and he doesn't want to go. His behaviour has nothing to do with what Gordon has said or done.

THE CHALLENGE: Don't personalise: it's not always about you.
Many situations are complicated and have more than one cause. Don't automatically assume that things are your fault or your responsibility.

Ask yourself
- ➤ Is this really about me? What other explanations might there be?
- ➤ Is this my responsibility?

Reflect
Can you think of a time when you were personalising? Describe it here:

5. MIND-READING

When we mind-read, we assume that we know what other people are thinking. Typically, we imagine that they are critical of, angry at or disappointed in us, even though we have no real evidence. These assumptions are often based on how we feel about ourselves, rather than what others are telling us.

Examples

CORY is self-conscious about talking in front of people. Whenever he has to talk in front of a group, he thinks to himself, 'They think I'm boring. They can see I look nervous and they probably think I'm weird.' (In fact, no one thinks this at all!)

ELAINE felt upset and embarrassed when she got lost trying to find her way to a friend's place for dinner. Elaine thought to herself,

'Everyone is going to think I am stupid to get lost like this. They must be annoyed because I've kept them waiting for so long.' (In reality, her friends were chatting away and barely noticed that she was late.)

THE CHALLENGE: Don't assume you know what others are thinking.

Ask yourself
> ➤ How do I know what other people are thinking? Do I have any evidence?
> ➤ Could I be projecting my own thoughts and/or feelings onto other people?

Reflect
Can you think of a time when you were mind-reading? Describe it here:

6. CATASTROPHISING

When we catastrophise, we exaggerate the negative consequences when things go wrong and we imagine that things are or will be disastrous.

EXAMPLES

RYAN went into a panic after he scored forty-five per cent on one of his assessment tasks. His self-talk went like this: 'I'm going to fail the year ... I won't be able to do any of the things that I want ... I won't have a future ... I'll end up on the dole.' While this assessment was a wake-up call, Ryan had passed everything else that year and was doing reasonably well, overall.

ALANNA was late for her Saturday morning job after sleeping through her alarm. The whole way to work she thought, 'My boss is going to be furious with me ... I'll probably get fired ... I'll never be able to find another job … I won't be able to go out because I won't be able to afford it, and then my friends will give up on me …' When she got to work, she apologised to her boss. He was concerned, but not angry, and he had no intention of sacking her.

THE CHALLENGE: Don't catastrophise!

Ask yourself
- ➤ Is my thinking reasonable, or am I catastrophising?
- ➤ If I was being more realistic and positive, how would I think about this situation?

Reflect
Can you think of a time when you catastrophised? Describe it here:

7. OVERGENERALISING

When we overgeneralise, we exaggerate the frequency of negative things in our lives, such as mistakes, disapproval and failures. Typically, we might think to ourselves: 'I always make mistakes' or 'My life is a mess'.

Examples

It took SAMARA quite a while to make new friends after she moved to another school. While she had made some friends at her previous school, Samara is now thinking to herself, 'I can never make friends.'

NICK feels very disappointed with himself for giving up on the saxophone after just a few months. He thinks to himself, 'whenever I try to do something new, it never works out.'

THE CHALLENGE: Be specific — don't overgeneralise.

Ask yourself
> ➤ Am I overgeneralising? Is this true in every situation?
> ➤ Are there situations where the things I am telling myself do not apply?

Reflect
Can you think of a time when you were overgeneralising? Describe it here:

8. HINDSIGHT VISION

Looking back on an event, we sometimes realise that if we had done things differently, the outcome probably would have been better — we have 'hindsight vision'. However, we cannot foresee everything from the outset.

Examples

STEPHAN chose physics as one of his subjects in the final year of high school. However, this turned out to be a mistake. He found it difficult and ended up spending a lot of time working on physics, at the expense of his other subjects. As a result, Stephan's final marks were not as good as he had hoped. Now, Stephan keeps blaming himself for choosing the wrong subjects and believes that he should have known better.

HILARY can't forgive herself for leaving her handbag unattended when she was at a party. Her bag was stolen and Hilary blames herself. She tells herself off: 'What a dimwit! I should have been more careful!' Now, with the benefit of hindsight, she can see what would have been a better strategy on the night (to keep her bag with her), but she could not see this at the time.

THE CHALLENGE: Have realistic expectations. We are always acting with limited knowledge and awareness. We can't predict and prepare for everything, but we can learn lessons for the future.

Ask yourself
> ➤ Are my expectations of myself reasonable? Is it possible to foresee everything that could go wrong?
> ➤ Can I learn from this experience, without blaming myself?

Reflect
Can you think of a time when your thinking was based on hindsight vision? Describe it here:

9. LABELLING

This is when we sum up ourselves (or another person) using simplistic, negative labels. Instead of criticising specific behaviours (e.g. 'That was a silly thing to say'), we write ourselves (or others) off with negative generalisations (e.g. 'I'm stupid'; 'I'm ugly'; 'She's dumb'; 'He's a loser'; 'I'm a failure'; 'He's a dropkick', etc.).

Examples

SHANNON *didn't know many people at a family friend's birthday party. Although she talked to a couple of people, she also spent time sitting on the couch, not talking to anyone. She left the party feeling down, thinking, 'I'm a misfit.'*

MIRA *had made a few mistakes at work recently, for which she was already feeling bad. Then, as she was backing out of a parking space in her father's car, she hit a pylon. Her thoughts became extremely negative and included things like: 'I'm hopeless and useless!' Thinking in this way made her feel worse.*

THE CHALLENGE: People are complex — don't label.

Ask yourself

➤ Is it reasonable to sum up a whole person with a single word or label?

➤ If I did something bad, or if there is something I don't like about myself, does that mean that I'm totally bad or worthless? Does this apply to others, too?

Reflect

Can you think of a time when you were labelling? Describe it here:

10. 'CAN'T STAND-ITIS'

Some people have a low tolerance for things they don't enjoy. Instead of accepting that life sometimes involves experiences that are difficult or unpleasant, they protest and resist, making things worse. They perceive that they 'can't stand' this or that, instead of just acknowledging that some things are not fun, but they don't last forever. When they can't change the situation, they suffer more by getting angry, frustrated and distressed about it.

Examples

> CRAIG *gets mad whenever he has do things that he doesn't like. He can't stand waiting in queues. He hates doing house chores and argues with his parents if they ask him to help out. If he has to go to a family function, he complains for weeks beforehand, and is often grumpy on the day. Most of these situations are not so terrible, but by being negative and inflexible, Craig experiences them as though they are absolutely awful.*

> DIANNE *hates doing things she doesn't enjoy. Although she is smart, Dianne loses interest very easily. She finds classes dull, and often*

takes short cuts with homework and assignments. When she doesn't understand a maths problem, she is reluctant to put in the effort to work it out, and ends up repeatedly complaining about how boring it is. This attitude makes things unpleasant for herself as well as others around her.

THE CHALLENGE: Accept that we can't always do things that are pleasurable, exciting or easy. Some things are not enjoyable — that's a normal part of life. Just because you don't enjoy it, doesn't mean you have to avoid it.

Ask yourself

➤ I don't like it, but can I stand it?

➤ Is it really that awful, or is my thinking making it worse?

Reflect

Can you think of a time when your thinking was based on can't stand-itis? Describe it here:

Look back over the various types of thinking errors in this chapter. Which ones are you particularly prone to?

As you become aware of situations where your thinking is affected in this way, stop and acknowledge the type of thinking error, and try to come up with a more reasonable perspective.

IN A NUTSHELL ...

➤ Thinking errors are categories of unreasonable, negative thinking that make us feel bad.

➤ Common thinking errors include black-and-white thinking, comparing, filtering, personalising, mind-reading, catastrophising, overgeneralising, hindsight vision, labelling and can't stand-itis.

➤ Whenever we find ourselves feeling bad or upset, it is helpful to check for thinking errors. Realising that our thinking is unreasonable can often help us to feel better.

FOUR

Tyranny of the 'Shoulds'

From early childhood, we start to make sense of our world — what is good and what is bad, what to strive for and what to avoid. Messages from our families, friends, teachers and the media tell us that certain things are valued, while others are not. For instance, being outgoing, intelligent, good-looking, hard-working and good at sport are generally considered desirable traits in Australian culture. Because we want to be liked and accepted by others, we take on some of their values and goals. We make rules for ourselves about how we should behave, appear and perform — we develop *'shoulds'*. This process starts when we are young and we are usually not conscious of it at the time. Although we may not be aware of our shoulds, we are probably aware of the distress that comes with not being able to live up to them.

The rules that we impose on ourselves are sometimes called *'the tyranny of the shoulds'*, because we become oppressed or 'tyrannised' by them. It is a bit like being ruled by a harsh dictator inside our own mind. Although it is helpful to have goals and ambitions, having unreasonably high or inflexible expectations of ourselves or others is usually unhelpful. Shoulds get us into trouble when we cannot fulfill them, or when the cost of trying to achieve them is too great. The cost may include emotional distress or an unbalanced lifestyle where there is little room for enjoyment. In pursuit of our shoulds, we may accomplish some things, but miss out on others. Good thinking involves having a flexible outlook. While we may try very hard to reach certain goals, we are able to adapt, and set new goals when some things don't work out.

> *TIM admits to being a perfectionist. If he gets less than ninety per cent on an assessment, he feels upset. If he makes a mistake, he dwells on it for days, and tells himself he is dumb and a failure. When he gets high marks, he feels happy for a while, but it never lasts long. Tim often avoids trying new things because he worries that he may not be able to do them perfectly. One night, Rebecca, a girl he has liked for ages, rang up and asked him to go indoor rock climbing with her on the weekend. Tim got off the phone and panicked. He had been rock climbing before and found it really hard. 'I'll look stupid and Rebecca won't want to go out with me again,' he thinks to himself. He also worries that he may not be able think of anything interesting to say, and that Rebecca will think he is boring. As his anxiety grows, Tim becomes very uneasy about the whole thing, and finally he calls Rebecca and tells her that he can't make it.*

It is not Tim's rock-climbing or conversation skills that are the problem, but his inflexible thinking. Tim believes: 'I should be able to do everything perfectly. If I can't, then I am no good.' While this motivates him to try hard in most of the things that he does, it is unhelpful in other ways.

First, it is hard for Tim to ever feel satisfied with his achievements, because he always has that niggling feeling that he could have done better. Second, whenever Tim fails to meet his own expectations, he feels inadequate and downhearted. Third, because he makes no allowances for mistakes or imperfections, Tim feels anxious much of the time. Sometimes his anxiety affects his concentration, making it even more difficult for him to get the high marks that are so important to him. Fourth, Tim is very cautious about taking risks, because he believes the consequences of failure would be catastrophic. This is why he turned down Rebecca's offer to go rock climbing. Finally, in social situations, Tim worries too much about making a good impression. When his friend asked him to give a speech at his 18th birthday celebration, instead of the usual nerves,

Tim was totally terrified and could barely speak. Tim hates feeling this way. However, he doesn't realise that his own unrealistic expectations (shoulds) are tyrannising him and holding him back, both at school and in his social life.

BECOMING MORE FLEXIBLE

Rigid, inflexible beliefs (shoulds) make us more likely to feel anxious, frustrated, inadequate, sad or angry, particularly when our experiences don't match our expectations. For example, if you believe that you *should* always perform brilliantly in all of your assignments, but you get an average mark for a particular assessment, you end up feeling discouraged and down. If you believe that you *should* always be confident and relaxed, but in a particular social situation you feel shy and self-conscious, you end up feeling doubly inadequate, because you believe that you shouldn't feel this way. Whenever we assume that things *should* be a certain way, or that we *must* achieve certain things, we put ourselves under enormous pressure and increase our likelihood of experiencing upsetting emotions. These can sometimes impair our performance and make it even harder to get the things we want.

Psychologically healthy thinking involves being flexible. While many things may matter to us, we don't see everything in absolutes. For example, self-talk such as 'I like to be friendly and supportive to others' is flexible, while 'I must always be supportive to anyone who needs my help' is not. The belief that 'It is important for me to do well in my school assessments' is flexible, while 'I must get top marks for all of my assessments' is not. The belief that 'When problems come up, there are usually solutions' is flexible, while 'There is always a correct solution to every problem' is not. 'I prefer to look good when I go out with friends' is flexible, but 'I must always look perfect' is not.

Of course, learning to be flexible doesn't mean that we should give up on our values and the things that matter to us. In fact, it is usually helpful to identify the things that are important to you (and within your control), and to work towards them. However, it is also helpful to accept that some things will not work out the way we would like and that, in the end, if we have to, we will adapt.

SOME COMMON SHOULDS

Take a look at some of the common shoulds below and put a tick in the box next to any that are relevant for you.

- ❏ I should be liked and approved of by everyone.
- ❏ I should always be successful in the things that I do.
- ❏ I should always do things perfectly.
- ❏ I should be thin/muscly/sexy etc.
- ❏ I should always look good.
- ❏ I should have a boyfriend/girlfriend.
- ❏ I should be the same as everyone else (I shouldn't be different).
- ❏ I should be confident, outgoing and have lots to say.
- ❏ I should be clear about my future and know where I am heading.
- ❏ I should always say the right thing at the right time.
- ❏ I should always be able to meet other people's expectations.
- ❏ I should always do what other people want.
- ❏ I should always feel calm and in control.
- ❏ I should always be happy.
- ❏ I should never make mistakes.
- ❏ I should always create a good impression.
- ❏ I should put other people's needs before my own.
- ❏ I should never say anything that might make other people feel uncomfortable.
- ❏ I should always make the right decisions.
- ❏ If there is a chance that something bad might happen, I should worry about it now.

Can you think of any other shoulds that are relevant for you?

CONVERTING SHOULDS INTO PREFERENCES

The trouble with shoulds is that they are inflexible. There is no problem with wanting or preferring things to be a certain way, and working towards that. However, when we believe that things *must* be a certain way, we set ourselves up for upsetting emotions such as hurt, anxiety, anger or despair. Becoming aware of our shoulds, and developing more flexible ways of thinking (from rules to preferences), improves our ability to handle potentially upsetting situations without getting upset.

Some examples:

➤ FRANK didn't get offered his first preference for a uni course he wanted to do.

➤ URSULA went out with a group of people that she didn't know well and she didn't say much all night.

➤ SHIRENE doesn't have anyone to take to her end-of-year formal.

➤ A girl made a negative comment to SAM about his new haircut.

In the above examples, these people could respond in different ways, depending on their thinking style. Let's take a look at their shoulds and some alternative, more flexible responses.

FRANK: 'I didn't get into the uni course I wanted.'

Frank's shoulds: I should always succeed. I should always achieve the goals that I set for myself. I should always meet the high expectations of my parents and teachers. If I don't, then I am no good.

Converting Frank's shoulds into preferences: I want to achieve all the goals I set for myself, but it's not always possible. Sometimes, no matter how hard I try, things will not work out the way I had hoped. It's disappointing, but there are other courses that I can do and different career paths that I can take.

*

URSULA: 'I am shy and can't think of what to say when I am with people I don't know well.'

Ursula's shoulds: I should always be outgoing and have lots of things to say.

Converting Ursula's shoulds into preferences: I wish I was more extroverted, but that is not my personality. It takes me a while to get to know people and feel comfortable with them. Once I get to know people, I usually relax and have more to say, but it takes longer for me than for others. I can still have friends and get on with people, even though I am shy.

*

SHIRENE: 'I don't have anyone to take to the formal.'

Shirene's shoulds: I should have a boyfriend, or at least one male friend that I can take to the formal. Because I don't, it means that there is something wrong with me. People must think I'm a loser.

Converting Shirene's shoulds into preferences: I would like to have someone to take to the formal, but it's not the end of the world if I don't. Quite a few people in my year are in the same situation and no one thinks badly of them. I can go and have a good time — in the end it's up to me.

*

SAM: 'A girl said something negative to me about my new haircut.'

Sam's shoulds: People should approve of my appearance. If someone criticises my hair, it means that I am not OK.

Converting Sam's shoulds into preferences: I prefer people to like the way I look, but I can handle it if some don't. We are all individuals with different tastes. If my haircut matters a lot to someone, it probably means they are very superficial. If it doesn't matter much to them, then I don't need to worry about it.

'OTHERS SHOULD ...'

In addition to shoulds that we hold for ourselves, we also hold rules about how other people should behave. Put a tick next to any of the following shoulds that are relevant to you.

- ❏ People should always be honest and reliable.
- ❏ People should always consider my feelings.
- ❏ People should share my opinions, ideas and values.
- ❏ People should behave decently and do what I believe is right.
- ❏ The world should be fair and I should always be treated fairly.

Perhaps in an ideal world, others would always do the right thing; however, we don't live in an ideal world. The reality is that people will let us down at times, or do things that we believe are wrong or unfair. The higher our expectations (that is, the more rigid our shoulds), the more angry or upset we become when this happens. It is reasonable to be disappointed or annoyed when people fall short, and sometimes it is helpful to talk to them about it, or to take some other action. In some cases, it may even be necessary to end a relationship. However, if we rigidly stick to the belief that 'Others should always do the right thing', we are likely to feel angry or resentful a lot of the time. This wastes our energy and distracts us from things that are more important. It might also lead us to say or do things that we later regret. (More about this in Chapter 6 on Anger.)

DO I REALLY WANT TO LET GO OF MY SHOULDS?

Even when people realise that their shoulds are unreasonable and make them feel bad, they are often reluctant to let them go. Many people believe that to get the things they want, they need to be hard on themselves. They worry that if they were to become flexible, they might not care enough, and so, stop striving to achieve their goals. The problem is that it usually doesn't work that way. Many of our shoulds are beyond our control and feeling inadequate for not meeting them does not improve things. Just because you would like to be slim, good-looking, confident, popular, calm, clever, outgoing, witty and dux of the school, believing that you *should* be this way does not make it happen. Even though you may have *some* control over certain things, such as getting good marks if you study hard, you rarely have *complete* control. While it is valuable to prepare, and put energy into things that matter to you, flexible thinking will help you to bounce back if you don't achieve your ideal result. Being unforgiving towards yourself seldom helps you in the long term.

Holding rigid shoulds may also leave you with hardly any time for other important things in your life (such connecting with friends, doing exercise, reading for pleasure, developing interests, etc.). The costs of being too inflexible may include an unhealthy lifestyle, unhappiness, social isolation and an inability to achieve other goals. (Remember Tim, whose unreasonable expectations made him feel inadequate and affected his ability to enjoy good relationships?) By all means, pursue your goals and dreams, but be sure to look after your other needs as well (see Chapter 14 on Self-care) and to be flexible in your thinking.

Reflect

Can you think of any shoulds that have caused you to feel bad in the past week?

Choose one of your shoulds that you would like to work on:

List the advantages of holding on to this should:

List the disadvantages of holding on to this should:

If you were to change this should into a preference, what would you be saying to yourself?

How would being flexible affect the way you feel?

Can you think of any shoulds that you hold about other people?

Are those shoulds helpful? Could there be any advantages in having more flexible expectations?

Now that you are getting the idea of shoulds, it's a good time to start identifying and challenging them in your daily life situations. To help you do this, the revised ABC Stress Log below contains an extra prompt, asking you to identify any underlying shoulds.

Exercise

Think of a recent situation in which you felt bad or upset. Fill in the Stress Log below, this time including any shoulds that you can identify.

STRESS LOG

ACTIVATING EVENT

BELIEFS/THOUGHTS

Shoulds

CONSEQUENCES
How did I feel?

What did I do?

IN A NUTSHELL ...

➤ Shoulds are the inflexible beliefs (rules) that we hold about how we, and other people, should be. The 'tyranny of the shoulds' refers to the upsetting emotions we experience as a result of holding onto these beliefs.

➤ Shoulds make us feel bad because our life circumstances do not always pan out according to our expectations.

➤ We can avoid upsetting emotions in many situations by learning to think in a more flexible way. This means that while we want or prefer things to be a certain way, we can accept that it won't always work out that way.

CHAPTER 5

Challenging Negative Thinking

One of the biggest problems with negative self-talk is that it always feels true. Even though our thoughts are often biased, misguided or incorrect, we assume they are facts. In reality, they are just perceptions. Often our thinking is skewed to the negative, and sometimes it is completely wrong. For this reason, it's important to keep an eye on the things we tell ourselves and to occasionally question them.

Our thoughts can be tested, challenged and changed. We can adjust the negative aspects of our thinking by identifying any unhelpful thoughts, then making a conscious decision to correct them.

> Although we can't always control the situation,
> we can change the way we think about it.

This brings us to the next stage of the ABC model, where A is for 'Activating Event', B is for 'Beliefs/Thoughts', and C is for 'Consequences'.

D IS FOR 'DISPUTE'

'Disputing' involves challenging the negative aspects of our thinking. By seeing things in a more reasonable, balanced way, we start to feel better. It also motivates us to behave in a more constructive way, consistent with our own goals.

Whenever you notice yourself feeling down, angry, anxious or upset, use this feeling as a signal to stop and observe your thinking.

CHALLENGING QUESTIONS

At times when we feel stuck in negative thoughts, it can be useful to ask ourselves some challenging questions. These enable us to check whether or not our thinking is reasonable, and can help us find other ways of perceiving our situations. These questions fall under three main headings:

1. Reality testing
2. Looking for alternative explanations
3. Putting things into perspective

1. REALITY TESTING

This involves looking for evidence (rather than just going by gut feeling) to see if what you are thinking is correct.

CHALLENGING QUESTIONS

- ➤ What evidence supports my thinking?
- ➤ Is there any evidence that *does not* support my thinking?
- ➤ Are my thoughts facts, or are they just my own interpretations?
- ➤ Am I jumping to negative conclusions?
- ➤ How can I work out if my thoughts are true?

JANE'S mum has been quiet and offhand for days. Jane feels upset because she assumes that her mum is angry or disappointed with her about something. Jane's thoughts include: 'She is mad at me ... She doesn't want me around ... I am a burden'. As a result, Jane feels down for days.

Finally, Jane starts to wonder whether she might be jumping to negative conclusions, so she decides to ask herself some challenging questions:

What evidence supports my thinking?
Mum has been quiet and offhand with me for days.

Is there any evidence that does not support my thinking?
Mum has still been making my lunches and driving me to the gym. She wished me 'good luck' for the swimming trials.

Are my thoughts facts, or are they just my own interpretations?
They are my own interpretations, not facts.

Am I jumping to negative conclusions?
Possibly.

How can I work out if my thoughts are true?
I need to have a conversation with mum, to find out what's going on.

That afternoon, Jane asked her mum whether she was angry or disappointed with her. What happened? Her mum apologised! She told Jane how difficult things had been at work recently (they had been talking about needing to sack some people) and how stressed she'd been feeling. She said she had been completely preoccupied with her own problems and had not even realised how shut off she had been. She was really sorry.

By checking out whether her thinking was correct (which included talking to her mum), Jane was able to recognise that she had jumped to negative conclusions and that the reality was quite different from her perceptions.

2. LOOK FOR ALTERNATIVE EXPLANATIONS

This involves exploring other ways of making sense of your situation.

CHALLENGING QUESTIONS

> ➤ Are there any other ways that I could look at this situation? What else could this mean?
> ➤ What would I say to a friend if they were in this situation?
> ➤ If I was a very positive person, how would I think about this?

When LUCAS recently failed his maths exam, his self-talk was: 'I'm dumb'; 'I'm a failure'; 'I'm not smart enough to be in this class'. Lucas felt very low and wanted to drop out. When he realised that his thinking was making things worse, Lucas decided to look for other possible explanations for his results.

Are there any other ways that I could look at this situation? What else could this mean?

I am not dumb or a failure, but I performed badly on this maths exam. This happened because I didn't prepare and because maths is not one of my strong subjects.

What would I say to a friend if they were in this situation?

I would remind him that, even if he doesn't do brilliantly at maths, it doesn't mean he is dumb or a failure. You can't sum up a person's intelligence by looking at just one exam result or one subject.

If I was a very positive person, how would I think about this?

I would acknowledge that I have always done well at English, history and art, so I am obviously not dumb. My talents lie in other areas, but if I put more effort into maths homework, I can do better next time.

3. PUTTING IT IN PERSPECTIVE

This involves 'de-catastrophising' — that is, recognising that our situation is not as bad as it might seem right now.

When we feel anxious, down or stressed out, we often expect the worst and automatically focus on the most negative aspects of our situation. When this happens, it's helpful to remind ourselves that our current emotions are making us see things in the most negative light.

CHALLENGING QUESTIONS

- ➤ Is this situation as bad as I am making out?
- ➤ Is there anything good about this situation?
- ➤ What is the worst thing that could happen? How likely is it?
- ➤ What is the best thing that can happen?
- ➤ What is most likely to happen?

AMANDA is prone to catastrophising. When things go wrong, Amanda reacts as though they are a total disaster, rather than a hassle or an inconvenience. When Amanda recently put on two kilograms in weight, she immediately thought that she had become fat and ugly, and that no one would want to be seen with her. When she didn't play particularly well in a netball game, she worried that she would be dropped from the team. When she had an argument with her best friend, she was convinced that their friendship was over.

Amanda knows that part of the problem is her own thinking. 'I get myself into a state about everything and I'm always thinking the worst,' she acknowledges.

Recently, someone posted a photo on Instagram of Amanda mucking around with some friends at a party. Now she notices that her dress had come up and her underpants were showing. Amanda is beside herself: 'OMG! How embarrassing! It's there for the whole world to see!'

After panicking for a couple of hours, Amanda decides to put things into perspective by asking herself some challenging questions. Here is what she writes:

Is the situation really as bad as I'm making out?
It feels pretty bad!

Is there anything good about this situation?
The photos of the party are full of people doing silly things, so maybe no one will focus on this particular one.

What is the worst thing that could happen?
People who see it will think I'm an idiot. I'll get a bad reputation.

What is the best that can happen?
No one will notice, and if they do, they won't care.

What is most likely to happen?
Some people will notice, but they probably won't dwell on it. Some people might think it's funny. It will probably be forgotten soon.

DISPUTE USING THE STRESS LOG

In earlier chapters, we used a simple Stress Log to highlight the link between As (Activating Events), Bs (Beliefs/Thoughts) and Cs (Consequences). This helped us to observe the way we respond to stressful situations. Now we come to the most important part: D (Dispute). When we dispute, we identify any thinking errors (see Chapter 3) and come up with more reasonable ways of thinking about our situation. Some of the challenging questions that we have just looked at can be used to prompt us to come up with alternative ways of thinking.

E IS FOR 'EFFECTIVE ACTION'

In addition to changing our thinking, sometimes we can also improve our situation by looking for solutions. Effective action involves problem-solving and might include things like looking online for more information, choosing to stay home on the weekend to complete an overdue assignment, apologising for saying something hurtful or seeing the school counsellor for help to deal with stress. Sometimes you may be able to solve a problem entirely, while other times you may be able to improve your situation to some degree.

Of course, not all action is effective and on occasions you might find yourself taking action that is *ineffective*. For instance, going on a crash diet to try to lose some weight, avoiding a difficult assignment by spending hours in a chat room, eating a tub of ice-cream in an effort to lift your mood, or refusing to talk about a problem when concerned friends want to help, are examples of ineffective action.

In the following examples, we will look at a few cases from Chapter 3 to see how to dispute using a Stress Log. We have also added an 'E', for 'Effective Action'.

STRESS LOG: RICKY

ACTIVATING EVENT	As part of my English project, I gave a presentation. Most of the feedback from class was positive, but two were critical.
BELIEFS/THOUGHTS	I wasn't good enough. I messed up. They didn't like it.
Shoulds	I should get a hundred per cent approval for my presentations.
CONSEQUENCES How did I feel? What did I do?	Depressed, anxious. I kept thinking about it. Couldn't let it go or focus on other things.

DISPUTE	
Thinking errors	Filtering, black-and-white thinking
Alternative, more balanced view?	It's unrealistic to expect everyone in the class to have the same opinion. The majority of comments were positive. You can't always please everyone. Some of the criticisms were actually valid.

EFFECTIVE ACTION	Review the comments that were critical and see if I can learn anything from them.

STRESS LOG: SHANNON

ACTIVATING EVENT	I didn't know many people at that birthday party. Spent some time sitting on the couch, not talking to anyone.

BELIEFS/THOUGHTS	Everyone else was having fun and talking to others, but not me. I don't fit in. There must be something wrong with me. People must think I'm a loser.
Shoulds	I should always be talking to people when I am at social functions.

CONSEQUENCES	
How did I feel?	Felt embarrassed, self-conscious, anxious.
What did I do?	Excused myself and went home early.

DISPUTE	
Thinking errors	Labelling, mind-reading, personalising, comparing
Alternative, more balanced view?	It's hard to be in a social situation where you know very few people — most people would find it difficult. Just because I didn't talk to many people does not mean I'm not OK. There are other people who know me and like me. I have no idea whether everyone else was having fun, or whether anyone thought badly of me. Chances are nobody noticed or cared.

EFFECTIVE ACTION	Next time I am in this situation, I will try to take a friend with me. I will also ask the host to introduce me to some of the other guests.

STRESS LOG: HILARY

ACTIVATING EVENT	Left my handbag unattended at a party. It got stolen.
BELIEFS/THOUGHTS Shoulds	What an idiot! This is my fault. I am hopeless. I should have been more careful. I should always be aware of negative things that can happen and make sure I prevent them.
CONSEQUENCES How did I feel? What did I do?	Feel angry at myself; frustrated. Kept thinking about it and telling myself off.
DISPUTE Thinking errors Alternative, more balanced view?	Labelling, hindsight vision I wish I had thought about the risks and taken precautions, but I wasn't aware of them at the time. I can learn from this experience and take more care in future. Everyone makes mistakes at times. I can't change the past, and berating myself will not bring my handbag back.
EFFECTIVE ACTION	Make sure I take more care with my bag in future situations like this.

STRESS LOG: ZORAN

ACTIVATING EVENT	My band did our first gig at the local 'Battle of the Bands'. Some people in the crowd were talking and not listening to our music.
BELIEFS/THOUGHTS Shoulds	It was a disaster! No one was listening. Our performance sucked! People should pay attention and show appreciation for our performance.
CONSEQUENCES How did I feel? What did I do?	Felt hurt, embarrassed, upset. Went straight home after the gig. Didn't speak to anyone.

DISPUTE	
Thinking errors	Black-and-white thinking, catastrophising, overgeneralising, personalising
Alternative, more balanced view	Many people weren't listening, but some were and others were even dancing a bit.
	Just because people were talking does not mean that we were bad. It was probably not about us. It is not the sort of place where people sit quietly and listen. It's a noisy hall.
	I have no evidence that our performance sucked, or that people thought we were bad. That's my own 'stuff'.

EFFECTIVE ACTION	Take every opportunity to get more gigs.
	Relax and focus on the music, even when people are talking.

CATCH IT, CHECK IT, CORRECT IT

An easy way to challenge your thinking as you go about your daily life is to use the 'three Cs':

1. **Catch** the thought: Notice what you are thinking right now.
2. **Check** the thought: Ask yourself: 'Is my thinking totally reasonable? Am I being negative, or making any thinking errors?'
3. **Correct** the thought: Come back with a more reasonable, balanced view.

It's that simple!

The advantage of the 'catch it, check it, correct it' technique is that you can use it anytime, anywhere, because it is all done inside your mind. For situations that are uncomplicated and easy to dispute, it is the perfect tool. Whenever you experience an upsetting emotion (such as anger, frustration, guilt, anxiety or the blues) you can use it as a prompt to think of the 'three Cs'.

For situations that are more difficult to dispute, the Stress Log is usually more effective, because writing things down adds a further level of processing. However, you can use the three Cs as soon as the situation arises, and later reinforce the disputing using a Stress Log when you have time to write it down.

BUT DO I REALLY WANT TO CHANGE?

Have you ever noticed that sometimes when you feel upset, part of you wants to hold on to those feelings? For instance, you might feel angry at a friend and a part of you wants to stay mad. Or you might feel guilty about something you did and a part of you wants to continue punishing yourself. Or you might become fixated on an issue that you can't control and, even though you know that it's pointless, part of you wants to keep thinking about it. Or you might find yourself behaving in a way that is destructive to you or the people you care about, and although you can see that you aren't being reasonable, part of you wants to continue. It is not unusual to have mixed feelings, where part of you wants to change and part of you wants to stay upset.

A variety of psychological factors can motivate us to *want* to think and behave in negative ways. Sometimes the 'primitive' part of our brain wants to experience unpleasant emotions because they feel helpful. (Remember, anxiety can motivate you to work harder, anger can motivate you to confront wrongdoings and seek justice, fear can motivate you to escape, etc.) The problem is that although upsetting emotions can at times be helpful, usually they are not, (especially as time goes on). Most often, they just make us feel bad. Their effect on our thoughts and behaviours can create problems in our school work, friendships and home life. So if you find yourself with 'mixed feelings', where part of you wants to stay upset and part of you wants to let it go, think about whether that emotion is helping or hindering you.

Here is a useful question to ask yourself:

Does thinking or behaving this way help me to achieve my goals?

For instance, do your current thoughts and feelings help you to have good relationships, or to improve your concentration at school, or to feel relaxed and happy, or to be healthy and energised? If your feelings or behaviours are moving you further away from where you want to be, aren't they self-defeating? Becoming more aware of the unhelpful nature of your current thoughts, feelings and behaviours can motivate you to want to change your thinking. With greater self-awareness you can refocus your attention on what really matters, and work towards those goals.

LEON had been angry at the world ever since his parents got divorced three years ago. He withdrew from his family and spent most of his spare time locked away in his room. Leon also became rude and sometimes aggressive towards some of his teachers, and even got annoyed with his friends. As a result, he found himself increasingly isolated. This caused him to focus on his own problems more and more, which only made him feel worse.

It was only when his school counsellor asked Leon a few key questions that he started to realise that his own thinking was part of the problem. His counsellor asked Leon what mattered to him the most. Leon thought about it, and finally said that it came down to three things: 'I want to feel physically well, I want to be comfortable with myself, and I want to have a clear head so I can finish Year 12.' His counsellor then asked, 'So if you continue to do what you are doing, is that helping you to achieve those goals?'

Leon began to realise that blaming other people and feeling angry at the world was not getting him what he wanted. It was making him lonely, isolated and depressed, and affecting his sleep, energy and ability to focus. This awareness motivated Leon to take greater responsibility for his anger and challenge the negative aspects of his thinking. He started making an effort to control his temper and be less harsh towards his family, teachers and friends.

PROBLEM-SOLVING

Some difficult situations are beyond our control and there is nothing we can do to change them. Other situations may be amenable to problem-solving. If there is something you can do to improve the situation, it is always worth exploring your options. For instance, although Leon could not stop his parents from getting divorced, he could make an effort to communicate with his family members instead of shutting them out. He could also stop isolating himself and spend more time with his friends. While these actions will not bring his parents back together, they are likely to improve his mood and make him feel better. (See also Chapter 11 on Problem-solving).

IN A NUTSHELL ...

➤ Although we can't always control our situations, we can learn to manage our emotional responses to them by challenging the negative aspects of our thinking.

➤ There are many different ways to dispute negative thinking. Challenging questions that encourage us to do reality testing, looking for alternative explanations and putting things into perspective can help us to view situations in a different light. (See 'Summary of challenging questions' below.)

➤ Sometimes we may find ourselves wanting to hold onto upsetting emotions. In these situations, it is helpful to ask ourselves: 'Does thinking or behaving this way help me to achieve my goals?'

SUMMARY OF CHALLENGING QUESTIONS

1. Reality testing

➤ What is the evidence for and against my thinking?
➤ Are my thoughts facts, or are they just my interpretations?
➤ Am I jumping to negative conclusions?
➤ How can I work out if my thoughts are true?

2. Look for alternative explanations

➤ Are there any other ways that I could look at this situation? What else could this mean?

➤ What would I tell a friend if they were in this situation?

➤ If I was a very positive person, how would I think about this?

3. Putting it in perspective

➤ Is this situation as bad as I am making out?

➤ Is there anything good about this situation?

➤ What is the worst thing that could happen? How likely is it?

➤ What is the best that can happen?

➤ What is most likely to happen?

SIX

Anger

Anger is that feeling we get when we believe that something is bad or unfair. We most often feel angry at people — parents, teachers, friends or even ourselves. While anger makes us focus on the injustice (the thing we believe is unfair), underneath it is a feeling of threat or vulnerability. This means that we feel hurt, unsafe or insecure.

Read the examples below and see if you can recognise the vulnerability in each case:

➤ *CELIA is angry at Suzie, who is her best friend, but was not there for Celia when she needed her support.*

➤ *MARLO feels angry and resentful towards his stepmother. Although she is usually kind to him, Marlo resents her role in his father's life and in the break-up of his family. He punishes both her and his father by being cold and withdrawn.*

➤ *GUS is angry because he perceives that his parents love his younger brother more than they love him.*

➤ *SIMONE is angry because her friend betrayed a secret that she had revealed to her in confidence.*

➤ *OWEN is angry because his little brother is wild and unpredictable, and Owen often has to look after him. Yesterday when Owen took him to the football, his brother threw Owen's phone across the grandstand and broke the screen.*

➤ *SANJAY has been wrongly accused of copying another student's essay. Sanjay is outraged — he would never do such a thing.*

➤ *ETHAN feels angry because he has been kept waiting for over an hour by a friend who is always late.*

➤ *LENA is angry because her parents are very strict and do not let her go out with friends on Saturday nights.*

A NORMAL EMOTION

Like all emotions, anger is appropriate and helpful at times. Anger motivates us to act, and can give us the energy and courage to resolve an injustice. Anger can motivate you to confront or communicate with someone, or follow up in some other way, when you believe something unfair has occurred. It also makes you feel powerful and can therefore override feelings of vulnerability or fear. For this reason, we sometimes like feeling angry and want to hold onto it.

On the downside, anger creates problems if it happens too often or intensely, or if it causes you to behave in a self-defeating way. For instance, anger might cause you to argue with friends, alienate other students or teachers, or fight with your parents. It can make communication difficult, and reduce your willingness to cooperate to try and sort out disagreements. It can also cause you to overthink things, and waste time and energy on stuff that is not worth stressing about.

EFFECTS OF ANGER

Anger affects us on three levels: body, thoughts and behaviours.

BODY

Anger can cause very strong physical reactions. When we get angry, our heart beats harder and faster, we feel hot and flushed, our breathing is rapid and shallow, and our muscles tense up. These and other changes are part of our body's primitive, hard-wired response to situations that are triggered by a perception of threat (that is, a belief that we are not safe). It is called the *fight-or-flight' response*, because it provides us with the extra boost of energy needed to either fight or flee. For our Stone Age ancestors facing a predator, the extra surge of power produced by this response helped them to survive (see also Chapter 7 on Anxiety). But for us today, these physical changes feel uncomfortable and provide no advantage, unless we actually need to fight someone or run away.

THOUGHTS

Anger interferes with our normal thought processes. It disrupts our concentration and turns our attention to perceived injustices (things we view as unfair). Sometimes we can spend hours going over these issues inside our mind (or 'ruminating'), even when there is nothing we can do. This is usually a waste of time, particularly when we could be focusing on other, more worthwhile things.

BEHAVIOURS

Anger often creates problems because it affects our behaviour. In a state of anger, you might argue, yell, withdraw, blame or shut down. You are more likely to behave impulsively and say or do things you later regret. In extreme cases, anger can lead to physical fights and property damage.

Anger creates tensions within relationships and may lead you to hurt people you care about. Frequent angry outbursts can make others 'walk on eggshells' around you, and even distance themselves from you. Angry interactions put people on the defensive, as they go into self-protection mode and discourage communication. When people feel threatened, communication becomes awkward or is cut off, so relationships are strained and problems are not resolved.

Some people express their anger through 'passive-aggressive' behaviour. This means they try to punish others by being silent or withdrawing.

Teenagers sometimes act in passive-aggressive ways towards adults to try to maintain some power in situations where they would otherwise feel powerless. So, for instance, they may shut themselves away in their room and only give one-word answers when their parents try to talk with them. Without yelling or slamming doors, passive-aggressive behaviour can send a very strong message to others that you are annoyed.

BRIEF ANGER EPISODES VERSUS LONG-TERM ANGER

Some people are 'hot reactors'. They fly off the handle easily, especially when they are stressed or tired. While their mood may bounce back in an hour or two, they can do a lot of damage in a short period of time. An angry outburst can destroy a friendship, get you kicked off a sports team, create enemies and make others lose respect for you. These brief episodes can be difficult to control and get you into all sorts of trouble.

Some people, however, can hold on to their anger for days, weeks or even years. They ruminate over injustices for hours and find it hard to let go. Anger occupies their mind and wastes their energy. This long-term anger can 'eat away' at you over time, affecting both your mental and physical wellbeing.

While both brief and long-term anger can create problems, the strategies we can use to manage them are different.

STRATEGIES FOR MANAGING BRIEF ANGER EPISODES

THE 'BREATHE–LEAVE–MOVE' TECHNIQUE

If you are a hot reactor, it is useful to have a strategy to short-circuit the response. Begin by recognising the *physical sensations* that signal the start of your anger. These are likely to include a hot, flushed feeling; a pounding heart; a clenched jaw; or trembling hands. Whenever you notice these signs, use them as your cue to think: 'Breathe–Leave–Move'.

Step one: Take a few slow, deep BREATHS, directing each breath into the lower part of your lungs. This helps to reduce arousal (your body's revved-up response) and refocuses your attention to your body.

Step two: LEAVE the scene, even if it is just for a few minutes. This protects you from saying or doing things you may later regret, and gives you a chance to cool down.

Step three: MOVE your body — do some exercise! For example, go for a walk or jog, go to the gym, ride your bike, dance to music or hit a punching bag. You can run up and down the stairs a few times if that is the only available option, but the key is to burn up some energy. Exercise is the most powerful way to control anger when it is 'hot'.

Once you feel calmer, you can then decide what you want to do. Perhaps you might realise that whatever you were angry about is not so important anyway. Or you might choose to take some action to address the injustice in a constructive, rather than a destructive, way. Either way, isn't it better to decide what to do when you are calm and thinking logically, rather than when you are fired up and furious?

DEAL WITH THE INJUSTICE

Anger may be signal that someone has done the wrong thing by you. Once your anger has cooled, you might decide that the situation is not worth bothering about after all. However, if you decide that it *does* matter, the next question to ask yourself is: Can you do something about it? Sometimes you can resolve an injustice by taking some effective action.

Take a look at the examples below. Under each example, suggest some action they could take that might resolve the injustice, or perhaps improve the situation.

1. ROWAN feels angry at his friend, who often borrows money but forgets to pay him back.

2. KAREN feels angry because she is doing most of the work in a group school project.

3. CON feels angry because his teacher claims he did not submit an essay, when Con knows that he did.

4. KAYLEE is angry at Isabella, because when they go out with Isabella's friends, she completely ignores Kaylee and spends her whole time talking to them.

Notice that in each example, communication is at least part of the solution. This is usually the case with resolving injustices. We get angry at people, so talking or writing to someone (either the one you are angry with, or a person higher up the ladder) is often the way to go (see Chapter 12 on Effective Communication).

However, we don't have total control over other people's behaviours and even good communication will not always resolve an injustice. We have all faced situations that are wrong or unfair, and there is nothing we can do to fix them. (Or we could try, but our chances of success are small, and it may not be worth the time, energy and stress.) It is not easy to accept things that are unfair, especially when they feel so wrong. But if you have to choose between long-term anger, or a brief period of anger followed by acceptance, which would you prefer?

STRATEGIES FOR MANAGING LONG-TERM ANGER

GIVE YOURSELF SOME 'STEWING TIME'

When you first become aware of an injustice, it is OK to 'stew' for a while (hours or days). During this time, it's a good idea to do lots of physical exercise. Also, consider talking about it to a friend, family member or counsellor. While some short-term rumination is normal, in most cases, anger fades with time. Usually, we eventually forget about it and our attention is drawn to other issues. If, however, you can't forget about it, and you continue to ruminate, it may be useful to consider some of the strategies described below.

DISPUTE UNHELPFUL THINKING

Anger is often fuelled by rigid, inflexible beliefs about how other people should behave. A Stress Log can be a useful tool for challenging some of those unhelpful beliefs, and developing a more balanced perspective. It also reminds us that there are other ways that we could be thinking about our situation.

> *JOHN had been excited about the camping trip that his dad had promised earlier in the year. Unfortunately, his dad suffers from depression, and a week before they were due to go, his dad cancelled the trip. He apologised to John and said they could go in the next school holidays, but John was too angry and disappointed to think about that. John stewed on it for a few days, then wrote his thoughts in a stress log.*

ACTIVATING EVENT	Dad cancelled the camping trip.

BELIEFS/THOUGHTS	Why can't he be reliable? He doesn't want to do things with me any more. He's always letting me down.
	What's the point of rescheduling — he'll just cancel again.
Shoulds	People should be reliable.
	When someone promises to do something, they should always do it.

CONSEQUENCES	
How did I feel?	Angry, disappointed, sad.
What did I do?	Sat in my room. Wouldn't talk to Dad for three days.

DISPUTE	
Thinking errors	Black-and-white thinking, overgeneralising
Alternative, more balanced view?	I wish Dad was more reliable but, given his illness, I guess he can't help it. People can't always be reliable.
	It's not his fault — he didn't do this to hurt me. I know he feels guilty.
	It's disappointing to miss out, but it's not the end of the world. Other opportunities will come up.

EFFECTIVE ACTION	I told Dad not to worry about it and to just focus on getting well.
	I will go bowling and to the movies with friends during the holidays. (It won't be as much fun as camping, but it's better than nothing.)

CHOOSE TO LET GO OF ANGER

When our anger is in response to unfair or bad behaviour by others, it usually feels totally reasonable to stay angry. But does anger actually help you, and how long do you want to be angry for? (Remember that anger can be helpful if it motivates you to take action or solve a problem. Beyond that, there is little to be gained from it.)

While anger wastes a lot of energy and attention, it can feel strangely satisfying. You might spend hours raging about some injustice and not want to be distracted from it. The reason is that *anger creates a feeling of power* at a time when we feel vulnerable and to release anger feels like you are giving up your power.

But is it real power?

VICKY and SAMANTHA both went out with the same guy, and both were cheated on and eventually dumped by him. Both girls feel angry, but Vicky gets over him quickly and channels her energy back into her rowing, school work and friends. Samantha keeps raging about what a jerk and liar he is, and how badly he behaved. She continues fuming for months. Samantha says: 'Why should I be the one to let go of my anger, when he was such a pig?'

How would you answer her? Which girl do you think has the power?

While it is normal to feel hurt and angry when you have been treated badly, remaining furious for weeks or months does not help the wound to heal. Ongoing anger does not stop feelings of hurt, loss or self-doubt, and it feeds overthinking and negative emotions.

Samantha is drawn to anger because it feels better than her underlying feelings of hurt and vulnerability. It feels like anger makes her powerful — but does it really?

Although it may feel like anger punishes the other person, it actually hurts *us*! Even if you can make the other person uncomfortable by ignoring them or being offhand when you see them, chances are you are suffering, too. Why do it to yourself?

Exercise

Think of a person that you feel (or have felt) angry at. What did they do that was bad or unfair?

Can you identify any threat, hurt or vulnerability that underpinned your feelings of anger?

How do you feel about giving up your anger towards them? Does part of you want to hold on to it?

DO A COST/BENEFIT ANALYSIS

Wanting to stay angry is usually the biggest obstacle to releasing anger. If part of you believes that your anger gives you power, you will naturally want to hold on to it. It is only when you realise that it doesn't give you power, and that the cost of anger outweighs any benefit, that you may feel ready to let it go.

A useful exercise is the 'cost/benefit analysis'. This involves writing down all the costs and all the benefits of staying angry. Let's take a look at Samantha's cost/benefit analysis of staying angry at her ex-boyfriend:

Benefits

> ➤ It feels justified — he doesn't deserve my forgiveness.
> ➤ Being angry sort of makes me feel good — like I am in the right.

Costs

> ➤ He's on my mind too much. The person I can't stand is inside my head all the time.
> ➤ All this rumination distracts me from thinking about other important things, including my school work.
> ➤ It upsets me — I get all churned up and sometimes get headaches.
> ➤ It stops me from getting a good night's sleep.
> ➤ It makes me feel on edge whenever I have to see him.
> ➤ It makes me irritable and cranky with Mum.
> ➤ It's such a waste of my time and energy.

After weighing up the costs and benefits, Samantha recognises that there is no real benefit but there are many costs in staying angry. Despite her initial belief that anger makes her strong, she now realises that, in fact, the opposite is true. Anger drains her energy, distracts her attention and makes her feel terrible. This realisation is helpful, as she now understands that it's OK to 'relax into acceptance'.

RELAX INTO ACCEPTANCE

When we are angry, we usually resist the idea of accepting the situation, even when there is nothing we can do to change it. Acceptance feels like we are giving the offender a victory — like *they win* and *we lose*. But is that really what happens?

Acceptance means acknowledging that the situation is not what we want or would like, but it is what it is. Once we can acknowledge that, we can relax into that reality.

When we relax into acceptance, we release physical tension and calm our bodies. We can think about the reality of our situation and make a conscious decision to drop any resistance that is inside of us. It's like the weather — you can't change it, so why fight against it? (See also 'Acceptance Affirmation' in Chapter 11 on Problem-solving.)

Exercise

Think of a situation that you feel angry about, but cannot change.

When you think about accepting it, do you notice any resistance?

What thoughts might get in the way of acceptance?

Note: In situations that involve bullying, it is absolutely essential to take action. This will include talking to your parents, teachers and the school counsellor and/or other senior teachers. Every person has the right to feel safe and treated respectfully in their school or work environment, and it is your school's legal and moral responsibility to make sure that any bullying behaviour is quickly stamped out. You should not be expected to live with or accept bullying under any circumstances.

APPLY GOAL-DIRECTED THINKING

Goal-directed thinking is a useful motivational strategy for releasing anger. Like the cost/benefit analysis, it helps us to recognise the self-defeating nature of our thinking. In this case, we remind ourselves to stay focused on the big picture — that is, our goals. Remember the question from Chapter 5: *Does thinking or behaving this way help me to achieve my goals?*

JIM is fuming because his teacher gave him a low mark on his history assignment. He believes it deserved better and has talked to his teacher about it, but his teacher won't budge. Jim realises that part of him wants to stay angry. But then he thinks about the bigger picture and asks himself: 'Does thinking or behaving this way help me to achieve my goals?'

He responds, 'My goal is to finish Year 12 with good enough marks to get into the uni course I want. Staying angry about this is a distraction and makes it harder to concentrate. It's not worth getting caught up in this stuff. I need to focus on my work.' Jim persuades himself to forget about it and to turn his attention to things that he can control.

FREDA feels angry at her friend Ellen, because she cannot make it to a gathering that Freda has planned. Freda feels like giving Ellen the cold shoulder for the next few weeks but then she asks herself: 'Does thinking or behaving this way help me to achieve my goals?'

Freda responds, 'I want to get on with people and have good relationships. Getting caught up in all these negative thoughts about Ellen creates distance between us. If I keep doing that, I will lose Ellen's friendship and I don't want that to happen. I am going to let this go now, but I might talk to Ellen about it at some stage in the future.'

By recognising that her greater goal is to keep Ellen's friendship, Freda convinces herself to let go of her rumination.

CHALLENGE THE SHOULDS THAT FUEL ANGER

We saw in Chapter 4 that upsetting emotions are fuelled by rigid, inflexible thoughts and beliefs, especially shoulds. This is particularly the case with anger, which is maintained by beliefs such as:

- ➤ Others should always do the right thing.
- ➤ The world should be fair and people should always be considerate and reasonable.
- ➤ I should always be treated fairly.

The problem with these beliefs is that they do not always match reality. The truth is, lots of things in life are not fair and sometimes there's nothing we can do about it.

A healthy approach is to try to fix the things when we can (see 'Deal with the injustice', page 53), and to accept the things that we can't fix. Remember the Serenity Prayer:

> God, grant me the serenity to accept the things that I cannot change,
> The courage to change the things that I can,
> And the wisdom to know the difference.

JUSTICE CAN BE SUBJECTIVE

Remember, too, that justice is often subjective (that is, based on our own, personal judgement). What seems fair to one person may seem unfair to another. Things are not always black and white.

WILLIAM is angry because he was not picked as captain of the school rugby team. He believes that he deserves it much more than the boy who was chosen. On the other hand, the coach has put a lot of thought into the decision and believes the other boy was better suited to the position.

CINDY feels outraged because she believes she was unfairly disqualified in the 200 m breaststroke race at the school swimming carnival. The pool official ruled that her stroke faulted at times, but Cindy is sure that it didn't. Two different viewpoints and both feel true.

ROSANNE is angry that her whole family has to make sacrifices because her elder sister is in Year 12. Her parents have set all sorts of restrictions for everyone in the family, including no TV before 9 pm, so that Rosanne's sister can concentrate on her studies. Rosanne thinks these rules are ridiculous. Her parents believe they are reasonable and, if they help their daughter to do well, it's a small price to pay.

TRY THIS BEHAVIOURAL EXPERIMENT

When we feel angry at someone, we often believe that there should be negative consequences for their bad behaviour: 'If someone does the wrong thing, they are a horrible person and deserve to suffer!'

Once we label someone as a 'bad' or 'horrible' person, it affects the way we behave towards them. We often want to punish them and make their life difficult. Typically, we might ignore them, be very quiet in their company, sneer at them, criticise them to others, or even make nasty comments to their face. The problem is that this behaviour maintains tension and bad feelings between you and them. Emotions like anger, resentment and hatred create negativity for you as well as the other person. Do you really want to keep feeling that way?

Here is an interesting behavioural experiment to challenge the belief that they 'deserve to suffer': choose to treat the other person with respect. Be pleasant and treat them as you would have others treat you — for at least three days.

Being nice to someone we dislike is often hard, because it goes against our instincts. Yet, it is a very interesting thing to attempt.

As this is an experiment, you never know for sure what will happen, but very often the results are surprisingly positive. Dropping hostile behaviour towards another person often leads them to change their behaviour and act less negatively towards us. It reduces feelings of threat and lowers the tension, which is often a relief for both you and them, so everyone benefits.

'But what if I am nice to them and they are not nice to me?' you wonder. 'Doesn't that mean that they win and I lose?' Not at all. You can always feel good about the fact that you chose to behave decently, regardless of their behaviour. After all, you don't need to let other people determine how you will act. And, you can always go back to your original behaviour after three days if you still think there is no value in change. What do you have to lose?

IN A NUTSHELL ...

➤ Anger is created by the perception that something is unfair and it is usually accompanied by feelings of threat or vulnerability.

➤ While it can sometimes motivate us to behave assertively or solve a problem, anger has many negative consequences.

➤ Acute, explosive anger is potentially harmful because it generates unhelpful behaviours that can alienate other people. Less intense but more sustained anger is also self-defeating because it drains our energy, impacts on our relationships and makes us feel bad.

➤ People often want to stay angry because they believe it is empowering. However, the costs of holding on to your anger are usually greater than the benefits.

➤ A number of strategies can help to release anger, including the 'Breathe–Leave–Move' technique, problem-solving, using a stress log, doing a cost/benefit analysis of staying angry, applying goal-directed thinking, practising acceptance and changing your behaviour towards the other person.

CHAPTER 7

Anxiety

Anxiety is that uneasy feeling we get when we perceive that something bad might happen. It feels unpleasant, because our mind is alerting us to a threat and our body responds with uncomfortable physical sensations, such as tightness in the chest, rapid shallow breathing, a pounding heart and butterflies in our tummy.

Of all the unpleasant emotions, anxiety is the most common, especially during our teenage years, which is not surprising as there are lots of pressures and demands during this stage of our lives.

YASMINE is sitting down trying to study but she can't focus. Her stomach is churning, her face is flushed and she feels tense and agitated. Her thoughts are racing; one moment she is thinking about her English assignment and the next she is thinking about her friend Lisa, who is struggling with an eating disorder. Then she thinks about her maths teacher's comment about the minimum entry-level scores needed to get into university, and then she thinks about sitting her final exams without being adequately prepared. In the end, Yasmine gives up on studying and goes to bed. But even in bed, her mind won't switch off. As the hours go by, she lies awake thinking about all sorts of things. Then she starts thinking about not being able to fall asleep and how terrible she will feel on the following day.

Although anxiety can sometimes feel a bit like torture, it is not always a bad thing. In fact, having some anxiety is normal and healthy.

BENEFITS OF ANXIETY

We feel anxious when we perceive some sort of threat and this can motivate us to take protective action. So, for instance, feeling anxious about having to give a presentation may motivate you to prepare a great speech; anxiety about an approaching exam may motivate you to study; and anxiety about not having started an assignment that is due this week may motivate you to get moving on it.

Anxiety also boosts energy and improves performance during high-pressure situations, like when you are working to a deadline, playing a competitive sport or participating in a school debate. Many people actually like the adrenaline hit that anxiety provides in high-pressure situations, because of its positive effect on performance.

Anxiety only becomes a problem when we experience it too often, or too intensely, and don't feel in control. Feeling overwhelmed by anxiety can impair performance and prevent us from achieving the things we want. So, for instance, Yasmine's anxiety affects her concentration, sleep and energy levels.

Once we understand how anxiety works — what causes it, how it affects us and what keeps it going — we can learn how to manage it better.

EFFECTS OF ANXIETY

Anxiety affects us in three key areas: body, thoughts and behaviours. Let's take a look at each of these.

BODY

The physical changes that accompany anxiety are known as the 'fight-or-flight' response. Our brain perceives threat and triggers the release of adrenaline from our adrenal glands (which sit just above the kidneys). This produces a surge of energy, increasing our levels of arousal and alertness, preparing us for action. Our muscles become tense, our breathing becomes rapid, our hearts race and our blood pressure increases. For our Stone Age ancestors, this response was very helpful, because it provided the extra energy required to fend off a wild animal, or to run away from danger (that's why it is called 'fight or flight').

In the very different world that we live in today, the fight-or-flight response is still occasionally helpful. As we mentioned earlier, it may give you extra energy when you are working in high-pressure situations. It might also help you escape potentially dangerous situations, such as when running from a bushfire, fleeing a would-be mugger, escaping from a vicious dog or getting out of the way of a speeding car. It may even give you a surge of energy when you are running for shelter during a thunderstorm!

However, most of the situations that trigger our fight-or-flight response do not involve physical danger. The threat we experience is usually to our emotional wellbeing, rather than to our physical safety or survival. So, for example, you might feel anxious about having to give a speech, doing a test for your driver's licence, needing to confront someone or going to a party where you won't know many people, even though you are not facing any risks of bodily harm. Therefore, being physically 'pumped up' and ready for action is unlikely to provide any advantage. In fact, it may have disadvantages, such as making you jittery, tense and distracted.

Ongoing anxiety can also result in uncomfortable physical symptoms, such as dizziness, nausea, twitches, headaches, tiredness, disturbed sleep, teeth-grinding and muscle spasms.

THOUGHTS

When we feel anxious, our thinking changes. Anxiety makes us more tuned in to possible threat. We are more likely to:

➤ Focus on the bad things that could happen
➤ Overestimate the likelihood that they will happen
➤ Exaggerate the negative consequences if they did happen ('catastrophise')

In an anxious state, we often get caught up in catastrophic thinking. We have 'false alarms' — that is, we perceive threat in all sorts of situations that are not really dangerous. We might worry about things that are highly unlikely to happen, or misinterpret neutral events (e.g. your friend didn't respond to your text immediately) in a catastrophic way ('She must be annoyed with me').

BEHAVIOURS

As mentioned earlier, anxiety can be a motivator. On the other hand, too much anxiety can reduce your effectiveness by causing you to procrastinate (keep putting things off), or to waste your time on things that aren't that important. In fact, avoidance is a common behavioural response to anxiety.

AVOIDANCE

Because anxiety feels unpleasant, we often try to *avoid* doing things that give rise to it. For example, if you need to talk to the school principal, resolve a problem with another student or make an uncomfortable phone call, you might find yourself putting it off time and time again. If you are very anxious about a school project, you might leave it until the last minute, and anxiety about who to ask to the school formal may cause you to stay home on the night. While avoiding these situations might feel easier in the short term, avoidance actually keeps anxiety going in the longer term.

Reflect

What sort of things do you sometimes avoid because they make you feel anxious?

What is the effect of avoiding them? Are there any downsides?

SAFETY BEHAVIOURS

Being anxious can also cause you to 'overdo' things, or to try too hard to make yourself 'safe'. For example, if you are anxious about your appearance, you might spend too much time in front of the mirror, trying to reassure yourself that you look OK. If you are anxious about your school work, you might spend much too much time on simple tasks. If you are anxious about some physical symptoms you are experiencing, you might research them online and create more anxiety by reading information about illnesses that are not relevant to you. If you are anxious about being liked by your friends, you might try too hard to please them. If you are anxious about meeting new people, you might ignore them in a group setting and just talk to the friends you know. These *safety behaviours* usually happen without much thought and most of the time we don't even realise we are using them.

> *ALEX tends to blush in social situations, and she worries that people will notice and think she is weird. When she is with friends, Alex tries to hide this embarrassing habit by standing or sitting in areas where there is less light. She often wears a scarf or high-necked jumper to cover up and, if she ends up blushing, she makes excuses to get away before anyone can notice. Alex believes that these behaviours are helpful, because they prevent people from seeing her go red.*

Recently, Alex has been invited to a brunch at an outdoor cafe and she can't get out of this one. She worries about being exposed in the natural light of the outdoors and, if she blushes, everyone will see. She plans to wear big sunglasses and a hat, so that at least part of her face will be hidden.

Exercise

What are Alex's safety behaviours?

What do you think is the effect of her safety behaviours? Are there any downsides?

If you were Alex's friend, what would you encourage her to do?

While most safety behaviours are actions that are clearly visible, some safety behaviours are performed inside our mind. These 'cognitive' safety behaviours include overthinking and overanalysing. Some people believe that the more they analyse and think through every possibility, the better prepared they will be. However, because they keep focusing on possible dangers, even when there is no need to worry, this process magnifies perceived threats and actually maintains anxiety. It also prevents them from focusing more fully on the things currently happening in their lives.

The trouble with using safety behaviours is that they keep us feeling unsafe, because they prevent us from discovering that many of the things that we fear are not really dangerous. It is only by facing our fears that we can learn not to be afraid of them.

Reflect

Can you think of any safety behaviours that you sometimes use?

What do you think would happen if you stopped using them?

STRATEGIES FOR MANAGING ANXIETY

In the rest of this chapter, we will look at various strategies that help to reduce anxiety and keep it in check. We begin with healthy lifestyle and communication, which are important for promoting good mental health overall, then we look at other approaches that are specific to managing anxiety.

MAINTAIN A HEALTHY LIFESTYLE

Our minds and bodies are interconnected. The things that happen in our body directly affect our mind and vice versa (see Chapter 14 on Self-care). When we make the effort to look after our physical health through things like healthy eating and daily exercise, we influence our brain chemistry in a way that improves our mood, calms the nervous system and increases our energy levels.

On the other hand, anything that reduces our physical energy will negatively affect our mental health. For this reason, avoiding habits such as smoking, drinking alcohol, taking drugs and staying up too late will also help to protect your mental health.

Physical exercise is particularly beneficial because it triggers the release of brain chemicals that make us feel more positive and reduce arousal. Any activity that increases your heart rate, such as fast walking, jogging, swimming or cycling, is beneficial. Regular exercise for at least thirty minutes a day provides the greatest benefits, but even small amounts can help to clear your mind and decrease tension.

COMMUNICATE

During times of anxiety or stress, talking to people can be very helpful. Friends, family members, teachers or school counsellors can be a great source of support. Sometimes they can provide reassurance and moral support; at other times, they can provide practical assistance. Sometimes they can help you clarify what you need to do, or enable you to see things in a more positive way. Different people can provide different types of support, but your willingness to reach out to them during times of stress and tell them what is happening is the most important thing. If they don't know what is going on, they can't help.

Reflect

Write a list of the people you could talk to if you are going through a period of anxiety or stress:

RELAX YOUR BODY

We saw earlier that when you feel anxious, your body becomes tense. But have you ever noticed that reducing tension in your body also reduces anxiety? Even your thinking becomes less catastrophic when your muscles relax!

Our brain is constantly receiving feedback from our muscles. Tense muscles inform our brain that we are still in danger, and this keeps us in a state of high alert. Relaxed muscles, on the other hand, provide an 'all-clear' message to the brain, causing anxiety to drop. In fact, it is impossible to remain anxious when your body is totally relaxed (although it is not always easy to relax when you feel anxious).

TRY PROGRESSIVE MUSCLE RELAXATION

We can achieve a state of deep relaxation by doing progressive muscle relaxation exercises — consciously relaxing our muscles, one group at a time. This process produces a much greater level of relaxation than you might experience when you are 'chilling out' watching TV on the couch. You create a state that is exactly the opposite of what happens when you feel anxious: your muscles relax, your heartbeat slows, your blood pressure drops and your breathing becomes slow and rhythmic.

Now you might be thinking to yourself, 'But deep relaxation will not solve my problems. I still need to get top marks in Year 12 to get into the uni course that I want', or 'I still need to get up in front of the class and give that speech'. It is true that learning to relax your body will not change the life situations you are dealing with. However, it *will* reduce the uncomfortable body sensations and catastrophic thoughts about those situations. Teaching your body to relax will allow you to think more clearly, and this will also make it easier to problem-solve, if that is what you need to do.

Progressive muscle relaxation involves sitting down and consciously working through a number of steps. The following describes the key steps involved:

> Find a quiet place that is free of distractions and loosen any clothing that is tight or uncomfortable. Sit upright in a comfortable position, with your feet flat on the floor. Place your hands wherever they feel most comfortable. Close your eyes and take a little time to get in touch with the sensations within your body.
> Breathe in and tighten the muscles of your feet. Hold your breath and tension for a few seconds, and then breathe out and relax your muscles. Observe the sensations within your feet as they relax.
> Repeat this procedure for all the major muscle groups, in the following order: calves, thighs, buttocks, stomach, chest, arms, shoulders, neck and face.

Now observe your whole body. Notice any part that is still tense and consciously relax the muscles in that area. Sit quietly for a few minutes and enjoy the sensations of relaxation.

While some people like to do this exercise by themselves, having the direction of a spoken voice can make it easier. There are many apps and online audio downloads, which provide guidance on progressive muscle relaxation. If you search online for 'progressive muscle relaxation audio', you will find many options.

DO A SLOW RHYTHMIC BREATHING EXERCISE

Slow rhythmic breathing can help you feel calm when you are hyped up or experiencing the fight-or-flight response (pounding heart, tight chest, rapid breathing, etc.). It is particularly helpful if you are having a panic attack. By deliberately slowing down your breath, you also reduce other components of arousal, including elevated heart rate and blood pressure. Here is a simple technique that is very effective:

1. Breathe in slowly (not too deeply) and hold your breath for a few seconds.
2. Breathe out slowly, saying the word 'relax' inside your mind as you breathe out. Feel yourself releasing tension as you say the word 'relax'.
3. Breathe in slowly again, this time saying the words 'breathe in' inside your mind. Hold your breath for a few seconds and breathe out slowly, saying the word 'relax' with the out-breath.

Continue to breathe in a slow rhythm, saying the words 'breathe in' with each in-breath and 'relax' with each out-breath.

If you prefer to use an external guide, there are free apps available online, such as 'Breathe2Relax' and Reachout's 'Breathe', which can guide you through slow rhythmic breathing.

MEDITATE

Meditation can be a useful tool for reducing anxiety and the unpleasant body sensations that accompany it (see also Chapter 10 on Mindfulness). While there are different ways of practising meditation, the most common involves focused concentration on the breath. (Other things, like sounds, a body scan or body sensations in motion can also be used as a point of focus.) By paying full attention to the present moment, the mind disconnects from the scattered or racing thoughts generated by anxiety. Some describe the experience as 'allowing the mud to settle'. Most people feel a noticeable reduction in anxiety after five to fifteen minutes of meditation, and the feeling may last for hours afterwards.

Unlike the slow rhythmic breathing exercise described earlier, meditation does not involve changing or controlling the breath. You just focus your mind on the sensations of the breath, in its own natural rhythm. Whenever you notice that your thoughts have wandered, gently return your attention to your breath.

Many people find meditation a challenging skill to learn; however, it becomes easier with practice. It is worth the effort, as it is a powerful tool for managing emotions. There are many apps and online audio downloads that can guide you in the practice (see Chapter 15 for more information).

PROBLEM-SOLVE

While anxiety is often created by catastrophic thinking, there are some circumstances that would be considered stressful by most people. Doing exams, meeting tight deadlines, needing to confront someone or attending a job interview are often anxiety-provoking situations. When you are faced with these challenging situations, it is helpful to consider problem-solving. Ask yourself, 'Is there anything I can do here?' Look for solutions, or ways of exerting some control.

NADIA feels anxious about a comment she made to her friend Vida, which she later realised could have been taken the wrong way. Nadia has been worrying for a few days and finally decides to take action. She calls Vida and talks to her about it. It turns out that Vida was a bit hurt by the comment, but after Nadia explained what she meant and apologised, the misunderstanding was resolved. Taking action to solve the problem enabled Nadia to put that issue to bed.

MATT is anxious about an English assignment, because he doesn't really understand what is required and doesn't know where to start. He talks to a couple of students in his class but they are not much help. In the end, he approaches his English teacher and arranges a time to discuss the project. This results in enormous relief, because now he understands what he needs to do and is able to make a start.

CIARAN is anxious about an upcoming interview for a work-experience position. He worries that he will sound dumb or say something stupid. Ciaran decides to do some research about the company, so he will be better informed. He prepares answers to questions they might ask and also prepares some questions that he would like to ask the manager. Doing this preparation makes Ciaran feel more confident and reduces his anxiety.

While sometimes the solutions are obvious, when facing more complex challenges, it may be worth brainstorming a number of possible solutions or getting advice from parents or teachers. A step-by-step problem-solving approach may sometimes be helpful (see Chapter 11 on Problem-solving).

WRITE A TO-DO LIST

Do you sometimes find yourself feeling overwhelmed by having so much to do and so little time? Here is a simple, yet very practical strategy: *write a list.*

At the start of each day, write down all the things you need to do, and refer back to the list several times during the day. Cross off items once you have completed them and carry over any unfinished items to the following day's list. Keeping a list helps you to feel in control, as you don't need to carry all those jobs inside your head. Crossing off items as you complete them creates a sense of achievement and is likely to lift your mood.

With very big jobs, it is helpful to break them down into smaller tasks. Listing each of these (e.g. 'Task one: …', 'Task two: …', 'Task three: …') makes the job feel more manageable and creates a feeling of achievement when you check off each task.

CONFRONT YOUR FEARS — AVOID AVOIDANCE!

Confronting, rather than *avoiding*, the situations we fear is one of the most effective ways to reduce anxiety over time. It is particularly helpful when we are dealing with *ongoing fears* that we know will not go away by themselves. These might include things like making potentially unpleasant phone calls, going to social events, approaching people in authority, learning to drive, spending time alone or starting a conversation with people to whom you are attracted. Confronting our feared situations helps to reduce anxiety, because we learn through experience that the situation is not so terrible. Even if it's difficult, we can cope.

So where to start? When the idea of facing your fears feels totally overwhelming, it's best to start with small, easy tasks and then gradually increase the challenge over time.

CHRIS is terrified of talking to girls. He would love to be able to chat with them, but he feels self-conscious and awkward around them. Chris wants to get over this fear, so he decides to start by briefly making eye contact and momentarily smiling as he passes some of the girls in the school corridor. He soon discovers that this is not as hard as he thought, so after a couple of weeks, Chris challenges himself further. Now he adds a 'hi', while passing some of the friendlier girls. To his surprise, he often gets a 'hi' back! It takes quite a while before Chris takes the next step, which is to start a conversation during a science prac class with one of the girls in his group. (He knows that they both go for the same football team, so he talks about the team's nail-biting win in last Saturday's game.) She chats a bit, and it goes OK. In the next prac class, he does it again, and it goes OK, except that he runs out of things to say. A few weeks later, Chris finds the courage to friend request her on Facebook, and to his delight, she accepts. Although he still has a long way to go, he has made progress, and this has boosted his confidence and given him hope. Chris now thinks about saying 'hi' to the girl he sees every morning at the bus stop.

The more often we face our feared situations, the less scary they become. If you are anxious about giving a presentation to the class, practise with your family or a small group of friends beforehand. If you have a fear of using lifts, start by going up only one floor at a time, and gradually increase the time you spend in there. If you have a fear of social situations, start with getting involved in lots of 'safe' situations (e.g. doing organised activities that bring you together with other teenagers) and gradually increase your exposure to other social situations.

Reflect

Are there any fears that you would like to overcome? If so, write down a number of small steps that you could take to confront those fears.

CONFRONT YOUR FEARS — DROP YOUR SAFETY BEHAVIOURS

As we saw earlier, safety behaviours are specific things we do to try to make our world 'safe'. These behaviours are driven by anxiety rather than rational decision making, and might include things like excessive checking, overplanning, perfectionistic behaviours, trying too hard to please people and reassurance-seeking behaviours.

RONNI was excited to be dating a girl he had had his eye on for months, but he worried that she may lose interest in him. To make sure she still liked him, Ronni texted and called her numerous times each day. Occasionally his girlfriend sounded impatient, which made him feel anxious, so he made extra calls to make sure she was still 'OK' with him. Finally, his girlfriend told him that his frequent contacts were annoying, and she would like him to 'chill'. On reflection, Ronni realised that his texts and calls were safety behaviours, driven by his fear of losing her. They did not make him more secure in the relationship – in fact, they were pushing his girlfriend away. Ronni decided to limit his contacts to three times a day (unless she called him first). Doing this enabled Ronni to learn that his girlfriend was still there for him and he did not need to spend so much time and effort seeking reassurance.

TRISTAN would get blind drunk whenever he went to parties and he then became loud and overbearing. At one party, Tristan damaged a wall and upset many people. After having to explain what happened to his parents, and pay for the damage, Tristan acknowledged that the binge drinking had to stop. Talking to the school counsellor enabled Tristan to realise that his drinking was a safety behaviour for dealing with his anxiety. His greatest fear was that people would see his social awkwardness and getting drunk enabled him to hide it. Tristan agreed to practice some of the strategies suggested by his counsellor to manage his anxiety. This helped him to discover that he was capable of enjoying himself at parties without getting blotto. Over time, his social confidence improved, and he could enjoy Sundays so much more without a hangover.

DISPUTE UNHELPFUL THINKING

In Chapter 3, we looked at the various thinking errors that lead to upsetting emotions such as anxiety, sadness, anger, frustration and guilt. Thinking errors that often play a role in producing anxiety include black-and-white thinking, mind-reading, catastrophising and comparing.

Whenever you find yourself feeling anxious, it's a good time to reflect on your self-talk. Remember, just because you think something, doesn't mean it's true! Writing your thoughts in a Stress Log helps you to break the habit of automatically 'buying into' any negative thoughts. Identifying these negative thoughts, recognising any thinking errors and coming up with more balanced, reasonable ways of seeing the situation gives you a different perspective.

THERESA is in Year 11 and has missed five weeks of school due to illness. Now she has returned to school, but feels anxious and overwhelmed by the amount of work that she needs to do to catch up. She doesn't know where to start.

ACTIVATING EVENT	Have fallen behind in my school work due to illness.
BELIEFS/THOUGHTS	I can never recover from this. I'm too far behind.
	Most people are on top of their work, but I am not.
	If I don't do well, people will think badly of me.
Shoulds	I should always be totally up to date in my school work.

CONSEQUENCES	
How did I feel?	Anxious, panicky, downhearted.
What did I do?	Procrastinated. Spent this evening messaging my friends instead of doing my work.

DISPUTE	
Thinking errors	Black-and-white thinking, mind-reading, comparing, catastrophising.
Alternative, more balanced view?	Other students take time off school for all sorts of reasons and they manage to catch up. It's not such an impossible task.
	Not everyone is up to date, even those who have not missed school.
	People understand if I don't do as well as usual, because they know I've been sick. No one is judging me (except me!).
	I prefer to be up to date and in control, and I usually am, but it's not always possible, and I can learn to live with that.

EFFECTIVE ACTION	Write down the specific tasks that I need to do. Break each one down into small steps.
	Start with easy, lead-in tasks for some subjects (reading and note-taking).
	Arrange to see each of my teachers and ask about exemptions for some of the work.
	Organise appointment to see school counsellor.

After Theresa finished working through her Stress Log, she realised that the situation was stressful but probably manageable. She then made a detailed list of all the things she needed to do.

WORRYING

While *anxiety* is our brain's response to perceived threat (current or future) and includes a physical response, *worrying* is a thought process. When we worry, we think about bad things that could happen in the future. Although it is normal to worry occasionally, worrying too much is unhelpful. It distracts our attention and makes it hard to concentrate. It uses 'nervous energy' and makes us feel tired. It also stops us from enjoying things that are happening now, because our mind is focused on possible future threats.

People who have a habit of worrying often feel driven to keep doing it because they confuse it with problem-solving; however, they are not the same thing. Problem-solving is a helpful process in situations where you are facing real challenges (such as Theresa, who has missed five weeks of school). It involves looking for solutions and implementing them. You can do this without worrying.

Some people believe that if they consider every possible disaster that could arise, they will be prepared for all negative events. Within their mind, they might start planning solutions to problems that *could* arise in the future. As the possibilities of things that could go wrong are endless, it is a pointless exercise. Good thinking involves accepting that uncertainty is a normal part of life, without overthinking and overanalysing.

When you think about it, just about every minute of every day, there is the possibility that something bad could happen, either physically (e.g. getting hurt) or socially (e.g. being criticised by others). Even if you are lying in bed going to sleep, things could go wrong. For example, a spider could bite you, you could fall out of bed and hurt yourself, or you could dislocate your shoulder when you roll over. The point is, the possibility that things might go wrong is always there, no matter what you do. If you spend your time worrying about all those possibilities, you become stuck in thoughts that are distracting and pointless. (And how do you know if you are worrying about the right thing?)

STRATEGIES FOR MANAGING WORRY

Here are some helpful strategies to help you keep your worrying in check.

PRACTISE MINDFUL AWARENESS OF THOUGHTS

Our minds are thinking constantly and most of the time we don't even realise it is happening. Mindful awareness of thoughts involves observing the thoughts that pop into our minds and noticing when they are repetitive, catastrophic or unreasonable. You can do this during a meditation session (simply notice where your mind has wandered to, before returning to your point of focus), or during everyday life situations.

Whenever you notice that you are experiencing anxiety, observe the type of thoughts that are popping into your mind. Acknowledge and label 'worrying' (thinking about possible future threats), 'ruminating' (repeatedly thinking about negative things that have happened and how you would wish it could have happened), 'overthinking' (thinking too much in any way that is unhelpful) and 'overanalysing' (spending too much time trying to consider every possible angle and consequence). Labelling your thoughts helps you to be aware that what you are experiencing is not 'reality' or 'truth', but thoughts — a product of your anxious mind. Notice your thoughts with curiosity and without judgement, a bit like an outside observer looking at something interesting. (What could be more interesting than the processes of your own mind?) Remember, too, that you don't need to 'buy into' everything that pops into your mind. Not all thoughts have value. (See also Chapter 10 on 'Mindfulness'.)

DELAY YOUR WORRIES

If you are a worrier, you might find it hard to stop, because worry feels protective (it is a safety behaviour), and to stop worrying makes you feel vulnerable. A useful tool to help you break the worry habit is the 'Worry Delay' pad. This involves noticing each time your mind gets caught up in a worry and jotting it down in a few words on a small pad (or mobile phone) that you carry with you. Once you have recorded the worry, make a commitment to drop it for now, but to come back to it at 7 pm (or some other time later in the day). If the same worry pops into your mind again, remind yourself that it is already in your pad and that you will review it that evening. Most people find that they can let go of worries, as long as they know that they will revisit them later.

What do you think will happen when the time comes to review your worries from that day? You might be surprised to find that the majority of those issues no longer feel important. In fact, often they don't even seem worth worrying about! If there are some worries that reflect ongoing threats to your wellbeing, ask yourself if there is anything you can do to problem-solve. Can you change anything about this situation, or is this something you need to accept? Does worrying about something that you cannot control make any sense? (See also 'Relax into acceptance' on page 59).

Delaying your worries is also a helpful strategy when you wake up in the middle of the night and can't get back to sleep. If you find yourself worrying about all sorts of things, write down your concerns and tell yourself you will follow up on these in the morning. When you look at them the following day, you may realise that your problems are not quite as serious as they seemed in the dark of night.

Writing down your thoughts is very important — just telling yourself not to worry about it now is not enough. Your mind needs to feel confident that this issue will not be forgotten, and that you will come back to it later.

If you prefer to do this using an app on your phone or tablet, Reachout's 'Worrytime' app can be downloaded for free. 'Worrytime' provides an easy way to record and store your worries.

EXAMINE THE EVIDENCE

When we are worrying about bad things that could happen, it can be helpful to evaluate our thoughts by looking at the objective facts of our situation, and examining whether the evidence supports our perceptions. The form below helps us to explore our thinking, using evidence rather than 'gut' feelings.

Examining the Evidence

Describe what you fear could happen:

1   What are the facts?

2   What are my thoughts about it?

3   Is there any evidence that supports my thoughts?

4   Is there any evidence that does not support my thoughts?

5   Is my thinking based on facts or my emotions?

6   Has my thinking been wrong before? How often?

7   Am I making any thinking errors?

8   What is an alternative, more balanced view? (Or, what would a calm, supportive friend say?)

On page 69 we met Alex, who has high anxiety about people noticing her frequent blushing. Alex is particularly worried about a coming brunch at an outdoor cafe. She decides to challenge some of her worrying thoughts using the Reality Testing form. Here is what she wrote.

Examining the Evidence

Describe what you fear could happen:
I could end up blushing (it doesn't take much), and everyone will see. They will wonder why, as there is no good reason. They will think I'm weird, and I will be publicly humiliated.

1 **What are the facts?**
   I blush very easily, especially in social situations.

2 **What are my thoughts about it?**
   People will notice when I blush and think I'm weird. They will wonder why I am blushing, as I have no reason to. They will think I'm crazy.

3 **Is there any evidence that supports my thoughts?**
   Not really, but I still think it is strange that I blush so easily, even with friends.

4 **Is there any evidence that does not support my thoughts?**
   I have blushed in front of people many times before and most of the time they haven't commented on it. I don't think they even noticed. A couple of times people have commented on it, but they didn't say very much and didn't seem very concerned. No one has ever criticised me for blushing.

5 **Is my thinking based on facts or my emotions?**
   It is based on my gut feelings — my emotions. I don't have any real evidence.

6 **Has my thinking been wrong before? How often?**
   I have worried about lots of things in the past and most of the time I have been wrong.

7 **Am I making any thinking errors?**
   I am mind-reading and catastrophising.

8 **What is an alternative, more balanced view? (Or, what would a calm, supportive friend say?)**
   Unless I do something seriously weird, like bark like a dog or stand on my head, most people will either not notice, or not care. I have blushed hundreds of times and no one has ever been concerned about it. For some reason, I am prone to blushing, but it's not my fault and it's not a serious defect. If I can learn to accept it, it's not going to bother anyone else.

After completing this exercise, Alex decides to confront her fears by dropping her safety behaviours. She will go to the brunch without any of her usual props. She is curious to see what happens when she faces her worst fear.

IN A NUTSHELL …

➤ Anxiety is that unpleasant feeling that comes when we perceive that something bad might happen. It is accompanied by physical tension and arousal, and it affects the way we think, feel and behave.

➤ Anxiety can motivate us to take positive action, such as studying for an exam or avoiding dangerous situations. However, too much anxiety can have negative effects.

➤ Useful strategies for managing anxiety include problem-solving, confronting the situations we fear, dropping safety behaviours, breathing and relaxation techniques, meditation, problem-solving and looking after our physical health.

➤ It is also useful to identify and challenge the thoughts that make us feel anxious. This can be done using a Stress Log or by examining the evidence using the worksheet on page 84.

EIGHT

Beating the Blues

We all have our down days from time to time. Feeling sad, low or blue (or what psychologists call 'depressed mood') is a normal reaction to upsetting things happening in our lives, such as problems in a relationship, difficulties with school work, pressure from parents or disagreements with friends. In this state, our thoughts become more negative and pessimistic. You might find yourself feeling particularly hopeless about things in your life, and solutions to problems seem non-existent. Usually, however, our mood improves after one or two days, or after a good night's sleep.

DEPRESSION

In some situations, we can become more and more down, and may end up getting depressed. Depression (sometimes called 'clinical depression') is much more debilitating than the regular blues, and has a big impact on how we think, feel and behave. Take Julian, for example.

After being together for six months, JULIAN'S girlfriend recently broke off their relationship. Julian was very upset, but he told himself that he would get over it soon. The problem was that he didn't get over it — in fact, over time, he started feeling worse.

When he was alone, Julian found himself feeling down and crying a lot. He lost his motivation to do things. He found it almost impossible to concentrate on his school work (which had always been important to him), and he lost interest in training at the gym (which he used to enjoy).

Friends would invite him out, but he just couldn't be bothered going. He didn't feel like being with people and even a quiet night playing video games at his best friend's house felt like too much effort. The only time Julian didn't feel bad was when he was sleeping, so he spent most of his time in bed and found it hard to get up for school. His parents and teachers were giving him a hard time, telling him to pull himself together. This only made him feel worse, because he couldn't see any way to do this. His thinking became very negative — it seemed that there was no point to anything and that things were never going to get better. Julian's negative self-talk kept going through his mind over and over again: 'Look at me, I'm a total loser ... I can't do anything ... I've got nothing going for me ... No wonder she broke up with me ...'

Julian's thoughts, feelings and behaviours are typical of people who are experiencing depression.

When people are depressed, they usually experience some or all of the following symptoms:

➤ Feeling sad, moody, irritable and upset. Crying a lot.
➤ Loss of energy — don't feel like doing anything (e.g. going out or talking to people).
➤ Problems with sleep (e.g. not being able to fall asleep, sleeping too much or waking up during the night).
➤ Disturbed eating patterns (e.g. loss of appetite or eating too much).
➤ Low self-esteem (e.g. feeling like you are worthless).
➤ Feeling like you can't cope with life — even the simplest things seem overwhelming and difficult.

➤ Becoming very focused on yourself. Losing interest in other things or people.

➤ Negative thoughts about yourself, and the people and things around you.

➤ Sense of hopelessness — feeling like there is no hope for the future and that things will never get better.

➤ Sense of helplessness — believing that there is nothing you can do to improve the situation.

➤ Sometimes, thoughts about self-harm or suicide.

Stressful life events, such as the break-up of a relationship, failure at school, being bullied or family conflict, can trigger an episode of depression. However, whether or not a person who is experiencing a stressful life event becomes depressed will depend on a number of things, including their early history, personality, thinking style, level of social support and current life circumstances. Some people also have a strong biological disposition, and are therefore more likely to experience depression (see 'A final word about biology and mental-health issues' on page 102). Things like having supportive friends and family, a strong passion or sense of purpose, and a healthy lifestyle can help protect against depression, or at least help us to bounce back more quickly.

EMOTIONS HEAL WITH TIME

When something bad happens or we lose something we value, it is normal to feel down for a period of time. Sometimes that feeling is grief, which is a normal reaction to a significant loss. If, for example, you are dealing with the break-up of a relationship, or if you have failed to get into a course that you had your heart set on, or if your parents are getting divorced and you realise that family life will never be the same, it is normal to grieve for a while. It takes time to adjust to unwelcome changes and to make sense of your new life circumstances. During this time, you may experience sadness, anger, frustration, guilt and low self-esteem. While you may think that you will feel this way forever, the reality is that these upsetting emotions will typically pass. Your circumstances may change, or, if they don't, you will adjust to them. (With time, we manage to adjust to most things.) During this period, the most helpful thing you can do is take care of yourself. This might include doing some daily physical exercise, paying extra attention to your diet (see Chapter 14 on Self-care), practising mindful awareness and acceptance of your emotions (see Chapter 10 on Mindfulness) and getting involved in activities that you enjoy. Spending time with people we like also helps emotions to heal. Usually with time, we start to feel better.

A major obstacle when we're feeling down is that we are often tempted to avoid other people and so we shut ourselves off from the rest of the world. The problem with doing this is, typically, the less you do, the worse you feel. Sometimes this can develop into a negative spiral, where inactivity combines with negative thoughts to further bring down our mood and motivation.

THE DEPRESSION SPIRAL

A depressed mood gives rise to negative thoughts, such as 'People don't like me', 'I am a bad person', 'Things will never get better', 'My situation is unfixable' and 'Everything is terrible'. These types of thoughts make us feel even more down, which in turn reduces our motivation. We feel drained, tired and like we can't be bothered doing anything. We might also assume that we are no fun to be around, so we avoid contact with other people and turn down invitations to catch up. The trouble is that when we avoid our usual activities, we tend to focus on ourselves and our problems more, and so we get caught up in more negative thoughts. (Remember, this is called 'rumination'.) As a result, we feel even worse. The combination of negative thoughts and inactivity can cause our mood to spiral down into depression.

The Depression Spiral

Trigger: Something upsetting happens
▼
Thoughts: Have negative thoughts about the situation
▼
Emotions: Feel sad
▼
Behaviour: Don't feel like doing anything or being with people
▼
Behaviour: Spend more time alone and become less active
▼
Emotions: Feel more depressed
▼
Thoughts: Have more negative thoughts
▼
Emotions: Feel even worse …

CLAIRE's family have moved to a new area, so she has had to change schools mid-term. Claire feels lost and alone, and has started feeling depressed.

The Depression Spiral

Trigger: Started at new school. Don't know anyone. Feel lonely.
▼
Thoughts: 'Everyone has friends except me.
I am an outsider. There is no one here for me.'
▼
Emotions: Feel very sad
▼
Behaviour: Avoided going to school last few days.
Spent most of my time in my room, either online or watching TV.
▼
Behaviour: 'I can't even bring myself to go to school. I'm hopeless.'
▼
Emotions: Feel more depressed.
▼
Thoughts: 'What's the use of trying? I'll never get over this'.

Reflect

If you have experienced a low mood or felt depressed recently, use the Stress Log below to describe what happened.

ACTIVATING EVENT

BELIEFS/THOUGHTS

Shoulds

CONSEQUENCES
How did I feel?

What did I do?

STRATEGIES TO PICK YOURSELF UP WHEN YOU'RE FEELING DOWN

As we have seen, one of the obstacles in trying to lift a depressed mood is a lack of motivation — you don't feel like doing anything. But remember the depression spiral — the less you do, the worse you feel. In the end, you may end up feeling terrible because you have achieved so little. All that sitting around also provides more opportunity to ruminate. For this reason, pushing yourself to do things, even when you don't feel like it, can make a big difference.

Whether you are experiencing depression or just a bout of the blues, it is useful to think back to the ABCs of your situation and do something about each of the three components: the Activating Event, your Beliefs/Thoughts and your Consequences (your resulting feelings and behaviours).

A. THE ACTIVATING EVENT: PROBLEM-SOLVE

A helpful question to ask yourself is: 'What is the best thing that I can do to resolve this problem?' Can you think of any actions that you can take to improve the situation? If you can think of something, make a decision to go ahead and do it. For example, you might call someone that you can count on for support, or decide to get some help with school work that you are finding difficult, or talk to your parents about an issue that has been bothering you.

For some problems, there are no obvious solutions and you may need to do some brainstorming in order to come up with the best strategies for dealing with them (see Chapter 11 on Problem-solving).

DOMINIQUE has been feeling very down lately. She bursts into tears easily and she doesn't seem to enjoy things any more. When she thinks about her triggers, Dominique realises that one of the main ones is the fact that her parents divorced about six months ago and she is finding all the changes associated with that really difficult to handle.

Dominique thinks about problem-solving, but she recognises that there is nothing she can do about her parents' divorce. Even though she would like them to get back together, this is not something she can control. So Dominique decides that this is one of those situations she needs to accept. What she can work on, however, are some of the specific problems that have arisen as a result of the break-up.

Dominique identifies two aspects of her parents' divorce that are particularly difficult for her:

1. Both her parents have been critical and negative about each other in front of her. Dominique has found this very upsetting, because she loves them both and doesn't want to take sides.

2. Dominique's parents have arranged for her to live with her mum during the week and to stay with her dad on weekends. The problem with this arrangement is that, while she likes spending time with her dad, he lives a long way from her school and friends. This makes it difficult for Dominique to catch up with her friends on weekends.

Dominique has decided to take the following steps to try to resolve these two issues.

First, she will talk to her parents separately and explain how she feels whenever they make nasty comments about each other. She will write down what she wants to say (using *whole messages* — see Chapter 12 on Effective Communication) and make a plan to talk to them both during the week.

Second, Dominique decides to bring up the issue of her living arrangements with her parents. She will explain why she is unhappy with the current situation, but also reassure her dad that it is important for her to spend time with him. She will suggest that a better option might be for her to stay at her dad's place two days during the week instead of on the weekends. If that isn't possible, perhaps she could spend alternate weekends at her mum's and dad's. Dominique is aware that her parents may not be able to change the arrangement because of their work schedules and travelling time, so she decides that another possible option might be to invite a friend to stay with her at her dad's place on some weekends.

By taking action to change the things that made her unhappy, Dominique was able to solve part of the problem. This made her feel better and lifted her mood.

B. DISPUTE UNHELPFUL THINKING

Our mood affects our thoughts, and our thoughts affect our mood. When we are feeling down or depressed, we think negatively about ourselves, other people and our future. Thinking errors such as catastrophising, filtering, labelling, black-and-white thinking and personalising happen without awareness, but they drag us down and keep us feeling low. For this reason, it can be helpful to monitor our self-talk and question whether it is reasonable. A Stress Log can be a useful tool for keeping our thinking in check. Let's take a look at an example.

EVIE had been trying all week to organise to go out on Saturday night. Unfortunately, the girls she asked already had commitments (a few had been invited to another girl's house, one had to babysit and the other had a family BBQ). Saturday night comes around and Evie is at home with her mum, feeling flat and lonely. She decides to use a Stress Log.

STRESS LOG: EVIE

ACTIVATING EVENT	It is Saturday night, and I have nowhere to go.
BELIEFS/THOUGHTS	I'm a loser! I've got no friends.
	Everyone else is going out and having a good time. I'm missing out.
Shoulds	I should always go out on a Saturday night.
CONSEQUENCES	
How did I feel?	Felt lonely and depressed.
What did I do?	Brooded. Ate a tub of ice cream.
DISPUTE	
Thinking errors	Overgeneralising, labelling, black-and-white thinking, comparing
Alternative, more balanced view?	There's no reason why I have to go out every Saturday night. It's OK to stay home at times.
	The truth is, I do have friends at school and I do go out on *some* Saturday nights.
	Staying home doesn't make me a loser. There is no reason to label myself by what I do on a Saturday night.
EFFECTIVE ACTION	As I'm staying home tonight, it's a good opportunity to go online and chat with my friend in the UK.

C. FOCUS ON BEHAVIOURS: STAY ACTIVE!

When we feel down or depressed, we normally assume that our problem is the bad things that are happening in our lives (e.g. too much school work, issues with parents, relationship break-ups, body image worries, etc.). But that is only part of the story. Once we feel down, a depressed mood and other negative emotions enter the picture. They affect our concentration, reduce our energy levels, decrease our motivation, affect our sleep and make us see everything in a negative light.

When we feel low, we often stop doing things we normally enjoy, such as catching up with friends, playing sport, going to the movies or heading to the beach. We just don't feel like doing these kinds of things — they seem like too much effort.

However, while these types of activities will not solve the original problem or fix a difficult situation, they can make us feel and function better. By turning our focus away from negative thoughts to the things happening in the outside world, activities lift our mood, even when the situation itself cannot be changed. This enables us to think more reasonably, see things in a more positive light and, sometimes, find solutions to our problems.

So the more down you feel, the more important it is to keep doing things. It may even be helpful to plan some activities every day, so that you know from the outset what you are going to do. At first it may feel like nothing is fun any more, but after a while you'll notice that your mood starts to lift.

There are two types of activities that are mood boosters: those that are *pleasurable* and those that give you a sense of *achievement.*

PLEASURABLE ACTIVITIES

Doing things that are enjoyable will help to lift your mood. Small things can make you feel better, such as walking while listening to podcasts, playing a musical instrument, talking to a friend on the phone, watching a funny video clip, looking at photos, listening to your favourite music or even having a bath.

Plan some pleasurable activities for when you are feeling down and remind yourself that this is the time to do nice things for yourself — guilt free!

Reflect

Make a list of pleasurable activities that you can enjoy at times when you feel down:

ACHIEVEMENT ACTIVITIES

Whether or not we are feeling blue, anything that gives us a sense of achievement will lift our mood. Examples of achievement activities include: making a phone call, cleaning up your room, doing some exercise, helping a friend, sorting out an unresolved issue, repairing something that is broken, writing an important email or completing some homework. Choose something that is not too difficult and, if you are able to complete it, acknowledge the achievement. (Remember, some things that are normally simple to do are often difficult when you are feeling low.)

Reflect

Make a list of activities that can give you a sense of achievement:

OTHER STRATEGIES FOR BEATING THE BLUES

SET GOALS

When we feel blue, we often get confused and lose our sense of direction. Our mind is not functioning clearly, so it is hard to know where to direct our limited energy. For this reason, setting goals can be practical, as well as mood-lifting.

Goals can focus on the short term, like something you want to achieve today, tomorrow or this week. Or they can focus on the longer term, such as something you want to achieve in the next few months, or even the next year or two. When you are feeling down or depressed, the most useful goals are short term, because these provide more immediate rewards.

You can set goals in different areas, such as friendships, exercise, school work, healthy eating, savings, sport, stress management, leisure activities, creative interests, meditation, etc.

It is always a good idea to write down your goals, as this helps to keep them in mind and reinforces what it is you want to achieve.

*ALYSSIA has felt down for several weeks, so she has set herself the
following goals for this week:*

➤ *Walk for half an hour every day after school.*

➤ *Ring my best friend, Emma.*

➤ *Make an appointment to see the school counsellor.*

➤ *Go to the football on Saturday afternoon with my sister,
Luisa, and her boyfriend, Angus.*

*After a few weeks, Alyssia's mood improved. She then set about
planning some longer-term goals. These included:*

➤ *Get fit enough to run in the local charity fun run in August.*

➤ *Plan a BBQ get-together for my seventeenth birthday in
November.*

➤ *Find out all the things I need to do in order to pursue a career
in journalism.*

Setting goals gives us something to aim towards, as well as a sense of
satisfaction when we achieve them.

When we feel low, even the smallest task can feel overwhelming. For
this reason, it's a good idea to set small, easy goals initially. If your goal
feels too difficult, break it down into small steps, then work through each
step one at a time. (See also Chapter 13 on Setting Goals.)

*DAN felt down about his school work, because he had chosen some
difficult subjects this year and has been struggling with them.
This caused him to sit at his desk and doodle instead of doing his
assignments — he just couldn't get started. Finally, he decided to tackle
the situation by breaking his assignments into small steps ('mini-goals')
and working through each step one by one. His first mini-goal was to
read five pages of chapter three of his textbook. His second mini-goal
was to write a brief summary of what he had read. His third was to
read over his summary. Getting started on some simple goals gave Dan
a sense of achievement and provided the psychological boost he needed
to motivate himself to work on more challenging tasks.*

PRACTISE MINDFULNESS

When practised regularly, concentration meditation can reduce distressing emotions and replace them with a calm feeling. This technique involves focusing your mind on a single object (usually your breath) and, as thoughts enter your mind, repeatedly returning your attention to your object of focus. Daily meditation can help you to manage upsetting emotions and allow you to experience this moment more fully, instead of getting lost in thoughts about the past or the future.

In addition to concentration meditation, one of the most useful aspects of mindfulness practice is *learning not to judge our current experience.* Whatever it is that we notice — whether it is negative thoughts, tension in the chest, or feelings of sadness, hopelessness or depression — we observe it with an open and accepting mind. Instead of trying to shut out those feelings, we allow ourselves to experience them fully and view them with curiosity, while remaining present and nonjudgemental. While this may sound like a strange thing to do, most people find the process calming. Very often when we stop trying to resist upsetting emotions, we give them space to pass on their own.

Mindful awareness of our thoughts as we go about our daily lives also enables us to notice the types of thoughts that keep popping into our mind. You might notice lots of 'to-do' thoughts, worries, rumination and specific problems sitting in the back of your mind. It is helpful to recognise that what we are experiencing are just thoughts, rather than 'facts' or 'reality'. When our mood is low, much of our thinking is negative and pessimistic, but they are still just thoughts and they will change when our mood changes. In the meantime, return your attention to the present moment — the things you are experiencing right now. A short time later, you may get caught up in more negative thoughts and ruminations. Once you realise it, simply acknowledge, 'Oh, that's more rumination' or 'That's my mind going to more negative thoughts', and return your attention back to what you are doing right now. This process of watching and labelling your own thoughts helps to disconnect from them, and gradually brings us back to the present.

In addition to thoughts, you might also notice feelings of heaviness and fatigue, anxiety, irritation, sadness and guilt. You might notice a heavy feeling in your chest, butterflies in your tummy or tightness in your muscles. Whatever body sensations accompany your feelings, try not to resist them but observe them with curiosity and acceptance. Relax into them and let them be. When we allow ourselves to experience upsetting emotions and sensations without fighting against them, they often drift away or transform all by themselves. (See also Chapter 10 on Mindfulness.)

COMMUNICATE: TALK TO YOUR FRIENDS AND FAMILY

When we feel down, we often feel like avoiding people. That is a normal, but unhelpful, reaction. Even though you may prefer to keep to yourself, do not give in to this feeling. You will feel better after you have talked to someone about your problems — ideally someone to whom you feel close. Talking to family members and good friends can be helpful, just because you know they care about you. They may also be able to reassure you, provide practical assistance, help you to feel better about yourself and encourage you to see your situation in a more positive way.

If you can't talk to your family or friends, talk to an adult you trust, such as your school counsellor, a teacher or your family doctor.

DO SOME PHYSICAL EXERCISE

Exercise stimulates the production of endorphins — brain chemicals that lift our mood and give us a natural sense of wellbeing. Regular exercise also contributes to healthy self-esteem and distracts from negative thoughts. If you aren't doing any exercise at the moment, try finding an activity that you enjoy. It really doesn't matter what you do, as long as it gets you *moving*. When you are feeling down, try to exercise every day, or most days. (See also Chapter 14 on Self-care.)

MAINTAIN A HEALTHY LIFESTYLE

Generally, things that are good for our physical health are also good for our mental health. A key example of this is a healthy, balanced diet, which recent research shows is essential for both mental and physical health. This means minimising processed foods and eating more fresh foods, especially fruit, vegetables, legumes and nuts. Giving up unhealthy lifestyle habits, such as drinking alcohol, smoking, taking drugs or not getting enough sleep, can also improve your mood and give your energy levels and vitality a boost. Do the right thing by your body, and it will do the right thing by you! (See also Chapter 14 on Self-care.)

PREVENTING FUTURE EPISODES

The following questions are designed to get you thinking about possible triggers for the blues or depression, the way you usually respond and some helpful strategies you could use in the future. Write your answers below and read over them every now and then, especially when you are feeling down.

1. List the kinds of things that might trigger the blues or depression for you in the future.

2. What types of thoughts have you noticed previously, when you have been feeling down?

4. How reasonable do they seem now? Suggest some more reasonable self-talk.

5. What happens to your behaviour when you feel down? What changes?

6. Suggest some helpful behaviours that you could engage in next time you feel down.

7. Are there any other things you can do to help yourself feel better (e.g. set some goals, do some physical exercise, do some activity, talk to someone, practise mindful awareness, etc.)?

8. Which people or services can you go to for support when you feel down? List everyone you can think of.

A FINAL WORD ABOUT BIOLOGY AND MENTAL-HEALTH ISSUES

Some types of depression are strongly influenced by biological disposition. About five to ten per cent of people who have depression experience *melancholic depression*, which means that biology plays an important role. (In these cases, there is often a history of depression in the family.) Stressful events may still trigger the onset, but sometimes it may seem like the depression comes out of the blue. This type of depression is severe and does not respond to self-help or talking therapy alone. Medication plus talking therapy usually achieves the best results.

Biology also plays an important role in *bipolar disorder*, which affects up to five per cent of the population and often emerges during teenage years. The depressive episodes that are part of bipolar disorder are usually melancholic, and therefore severe. In addition to depression, the person may experience occasional periods (a few days or more) where they feel energised, charged or wired, and have little need to sleep. During this time, they may be extremely productive, full of ideas and confident that they will succeed. While people in this state usually feel good, they may also feel irritable and become argumentative. Some people who have bipolar disorder are not correctly diagnosed for many years, which is a problem because accurate diagnosis is important for effective treatment.

About three per cent of people experience a psychotic episode at some time in their lives. The first episode often occurs during the late teenage years or early twenties and may be triggered by drugs (like ice or marijuana) or severe stress. The episode may be part of an underlying illness, such as schizophrenia or bipolar disorder, or it may be a single episode that does not occur again. The likelihood of a psychotic episode increases if the person already has a biological predisposition.

During a psychotic episode, a person loses touch with reality. They may experience delusions (false beliefs, e.g. thinking special agents are stalking them or that they have magic powers), hallucinations (e.g. seeing, hearing and/or feeling things that don't exist) and confused thinking (e.g. not being able to concentrate or follow conversations, or speaking in a way that doesn't make sense). They may also behave strangely (e.g. laughing at something that is not funny).

As with melancholic depression and bipolar disorder, psychotic illness is usually treated with medication, in combination with talking therapy.

If you are experiencing any of the symptoms described here, it is vital to talk to a mental-health professional (a school counsellor, psychologist or psychiatrist). They will conduct an assessment, explain what is going on and recommend the best strategy to manage your symptoms.

SEEK EXTRA HELP

Whether depression is caused largely by psychological or biological factors, it is often difficult to manage on your own. While the strategies described in this book may be helpful, they are often hard to implement when you are depressed. If you find it difficult to do simple things like get out of bed or go to school, or if you find yourself thinking about suicide or harming yourself, it is essential to tell someone you trust and get help right away. Talk to your parents, a teacher, your school counsellor or your GP about how you feel. Ask your GP to recommend a psychologist or psychiatrist who you can talk to you about your situation.

You can also call one of the following telephone help services: Kids Helpline 1800 551 800 or Lifeline 13 11 14.

IN A NUTSHELL ...

➤ Sadness or 'the blues' are normal reactions to things that go wrong in our lives. Depression is more intense and long-lasting, and can affect our motivation, appetite, sleep, concentration and ability to make decisions.

➤ When you feel down or depressed, it is important to keep doing things — talk to people and stay active. Staying in bed or watching TV for hours only makes you feel worse.

➤ Other helpful strategies include problem-solving, physical exercise, setting goals and challenging the negative, self-defeating thoughts that keep you feeling low.

➤ Depression is not something that you can just 'snap out of'. If you are feeling depressed, it is important to talk to someone about it, such as your parents, a teacher, a counsellor or your doctor.

NINE

Self-esteem

We all have times when we feel bad about ourselves. It may be a lack of confidence when you see a photo of yourself and you don't look the way you would like. Or self-doubt may creep in after a friendship ends, or a boyfriend or girlfriend breaks up with you. You might find yourself wondering, 'Is there something wrong with me?'

As a teenager, it is common to go through periods of questioning: 'Am I good enough? How do I compare with others?' With all the physical, emotional and social changes happening, it's no wonder many teenagers have ups and downs in the way they view themselves. Questions about identity, such as 'Who am I really?' and 'Where do I fit in?', are common. While most teens don't like aspects of themselves at times, the term 'self-esteem' refers to something broader.

Our self-esteem is the way we think and feel about ourselves as a person. It is the way we perceive our own worth. If you have healthy self-esteem, you believe that you are as 'OK' as everyone else. Low self-esteem means feeling 'not OK' — it is a sense that you are not as good as others, or that you don't measure up. People with low self-esteem tend to focus on and magnify their perceived faults and weaknesses, and ignore their strengths and positive qualities. It's like looking in the mirror and seeing a warped picture — a bit like the ones at fun parks that make you look distorted.

RICKI'S self-talk is constant put-downs. He often tells himself that he is ugly, that he sounds dumb and that no one could possibly like him. He is always comparing himself to others and ends up feeling not good enough: ('That guy is so much better looking than me; why would anyone be interested in me?'). While he criticises himself a lot, he hardly ever acknowledges his positive features. Whenever things go well for him, Ricki tells himself it was just luck or a fluke — he never gives himself any credit! The strange thing is that Ricki is quite likeable, but he doesn't see it.

FACTORS THAT INFLUENCE SELF-ESTEEM

The way that we perceive ourselves is influenced by our temperament, as well as the many things that we have experienced from early childhood right up to our present.

TEMPERAMENT

Our temperament is the part of our personality that we were born with; it is a product of our biology, rather than our environment. This includes things like how strong our emotional reactions are, whether we are shy or outgoing, our willingness to persist with things and how easily we become anxious or irritable. Our temperament can affect how we respond to situations and how we engage with others. This can influence the way we come to see ourselves. For example, someone who is shy or inhibited by nature might have fewer positive interactions with others, because they tend to keep to themselves. An irritable temperament may lead to conflicts with others, which may affect the quality of a person's relationships. Someone who is prone to negative emotional reactions may perceive themselves as inadequate when they compare themselves to others.

LIFE EXPERIENCES

Emotional or physical neglect or abuse during childhood can negatively affect the way we perceive ourselves now. Such experiences can lead to beliefs like: 'I am unlovable', 'I deserve to be punished' or 'There is something wrong with me'.

If the way you perceive yourself has been influenced by such events, it would be helpful to address these issues. Making sense of the factors that have had an impact on the way you see yourself is important for wounds to heal. If you are in this situation, reach out for support from a trained professional such as a school counsellor, psychologist or psychiatrist. Talking to a professional can help you make sense of what happened. It can also enable you to more fully understand that the responsibility for whatever occurred in the past belongs with the people who had power over you at that time.

SOCIAL INFLUENCES

The way we feel about ourselves can be influenced by how we interact with other people and the way they treat us.

FAMILY DYNAMICS

From early on in our lives, we develop a sense of who we are through our relationships with people in our 'inner circle'. Family dynamics — the way we interact with our parents, siblings and other family members — shape our sense of self. Being nurtured, cared for and loved unconditionally (even when you do something wrong) gives you the message 'I'm lovable — I'm OK'. On the other hand, parents with unrealistically high expectations, or who repeatedly criticise or negatively compare you to others, can give you the message that you are not good enough. Family situations where you are rarely encouraged or given attention, or where you feel left out or completely controlled, can lead to the development of negative self-beliefs, such as, 'I'm not good enough', 'I'm not important' or 'I'm a failure'. A family situation where there is constant conflict or a bitter break-up can also affect your beliefs about yourself, especially if you blame yourself. When we are young, it can be hard to understand these are the adults' own issues, and not our fault or responsibility.

PEER RELATIONSHIPS

During adolescence, our relationships with friends take on an increasingly important role. As we strive to develop a sense of who we are and where we fit, we rely on interactions with friends for feedback. Feeling accepted, valued and part of the group can enhance self-esteem, as we get the message 'I'm OK — I belong'. Alternatively, being rejected, isolated or unwanted sends the opposite message, and can diminish our self-esteem.

TAJ has been part of a core group of friends for years. However, since the beginning of high school, he has been feeling less connected to them. They have begun hanging out with another group at lunchtime, and Taj doesn't feel comfortable with these boys. They are into parties and meeting girls, but this is not his scene. When Taj tries to talk to his friends about his passion for film-making and the music that he likes, they make fun of his 'weird' tastes. Taj feels pressured to go along with what they consider 'cool'. Over time, he gets very down on himself, as he believes, 'I'm the odd one out. There is something wrong with me.'

SASKIA is struggling socially. Since changing schools, it has been hard for her to find a group of friends that she clicks with. In her mind, she is so different from the other girls at her school. They seem smarter and more outgoing than her; they wear the latest trends, and get up to all sorts of fun things on the weekends. Saskia doesn't get invited to their social events and feels awkward about finding people to hang out with at school. She tells herself: 'I don't fit in.'

BODY IMAGE

The way we perceive our appearance can influence our self-esteem, especially during teenage years. 'Body image' is the way you think and feel about the way you look. Negative body image is more than just feeling a bit self-conscious about your appearance. It is general dissatisfaction and unhappiness with your body and looks.

Given all the physical changes that happen during adolescence, and our growing desire to fit in, it is not surprising that many teenagers struggle with the way they look. Body image is often an issue for girls and boys who develop much earlier or later than their friends or peers. For example, if you're a girl who has already gone through puberty, you might feel self-conscious about having breasts or your period, if most other girls your age don't. Likewise, boys who don't start developing until later than most of their peers may compare themselves negatively to others their age who develop a more 'adult' physique earlier on. Other changes that often occur in puberty, such as gaining weight or getting pimples, can also affect self-esteem.

BEN has acne-prone skin. He constantly compares himself to other boys he sees around, and good-looking guys portrayed in the media. They all have clear skin! Whenever ads for pimple treatments come on TV, his attention is drawn to the images of people with pimples looking unhappy and alone, whereas those with clear skin are portrayed as having lots of fun, surrounded by friends and looking confident. He develops the belief that 'I am ugly and inferior'.

MEDIA MESSAGES

Every day we are exposed to messages about how we should be, look and act, and what we should achieve in order to be considered a 'success'. There are the Year 12 'high achievers' lists in the newspaper (sending the message that being a top student equals success), and individuals are held up as heroes because of their sporting achievements or how attractive they are. On social media, people earn status based on the number of 'followers', 'friends' or 'likes' they have, and celebrities portray their seemingly perfect lives through stage-managed stories (conveying the idea that 'If you are beautiful or talented like me, you can be happy and have it all!').

Underlying these messages is the theme: 'Everyone is doing better than me!' If we buy into these messages without questioning them, we can end up feeling inadequate. The truth is that social media provides an incomplete, biased and unrealistic impression of other people's lives, so be a critical consumer and take what you see there with a grain of salt.

SOCIETY'S NORMS

If we perceive that we are not included, valued or respected by the broader community, this can make us feel like an outsider, which can have a negative impact on our self-esteem.

> *AMARA is from a Muslim background. She lives in an area where there are very few Muslim families, and at school she is the only girl who wears a hijab. Amara is aware that people often look at her. When she goes to the shops, to restaurants or on public transport, she feels that people treat her differently and she worries they are making negative assumptions about her. This makes her feel uncomfortable and she often feels like she doesn't fit in.*

> *JOHN has known that he was attracted to other males from a young age. He is passionate about playing football, but around the club and among his team-mates there are constantly jokes and belittling comments made about gay people. At school, boys often use labels such as 'homo' and 'gay' as put-downs, and his family attends a church group that views homosexuality as a 'sin'. John views himself as 'immoral' and 'unacceptable' due to his sexuality.*

Reflect

It can be helpful to try to identify and understand any factors (either current or from the past) which may have had an impact on your self-esteem. List any that come to mind.

EFFECTS OF LOW SELF-ESTEEM

Low self-esteem can influence various aspects of our lives: how we feel, how we behave in relation to others and how we take care of ourselves. Below are some of the common behaviours that are related to low self-esteem.

TRYING TOO HARD TO PLEASE OTHERS

Feeling like we're not good enough affects the way we behave with other people. For instance, you might find yourself being unassertive (not saying what you think, feel or want), and trying too hard to please others. You might be too keen to go along with things, regardless of what you really think, or you might find it hard to say 'no' to requests from others, because you worry that they won't like you. If you believe you have nothing to offer, you may try to earn other people's friendship by doing favours for them, or allowing them to 'walk all over you'.

> *ELI has always had a low opinion of himself. He is shy and was bullied at primary school. Now he continues to experience difficulties with friendships, because he is always assuming that no one would like him if he is himself. As a result, whenever he meets new people, he bends over backwards to please them. He agrees with them about everything, goes along with whatever they ask and tries to imitate their dress style, haircuts and interests. Unfortunately, people find his behaviour annoying and many try to distance themselves from him. This perceived rejection makes Eli feel more inadequate, which makes him try even harder.*

PERFECTIONISM

Feeling defective motivates some people to strive to be the very best in one or several areas. Perfectionism is often a way of trying to compensate for perceived inadequacies.

While working towards an important goal or aiming for excellence is often positive and worthwhile, at the extreme end, excessively high standards are usually problematic. Perfectionistic attitudes come without flexibility, because we believe that things *must* be perfect. This creates anxiety and makes it hard to feel satisfied with your achievements, as they could always have been better. In striving for perfection, you may spend too much time on particular tasks and allocate little time for other important things, such as exercise, seeing friends, relaxation, reading and other leisure activities. The unbalanced lifestyle that this creates is not psychologically healthy and may leave you feeling lonely and dissatisfied.

TEAGAN has always felt inadequate. She sets herself unrealistic expectations and is very hard on herself when she fails to meet them. Teagan believes: 'I must get above ninety-five per cent in everything,' and she studies late into the night, and all weekends and holidays, to try to achieve this. She feels under huge pressure and is often exhausted. If she doesn't meet her own expectations, she feels like a failure. Even when she does, she feels momentarily relieved but then begins stressing about the next task. Teagan's perfectionism extends to many other areas, including her sports performance, her clothes and her weight. This leaves her unable to relax, as she believes there is always more that she could be doing. Although Teagan's perfectionistic standards are the result of low self-esteem (she is constantly trying to prove her worth), they also maintain the problem, as she never feels good enough.

LOW SELF-CARE

If you believe 'I don't matter' or 'I'm not important', this can affect your willingness to take care of yourself. For instance, you might see no point in eating well, or doing regular exercise or nice things for yourself. Feelings of worthlessness cause some people to put themselves in situations where they are not treated with respect, or engage in behaviours where their safety or wellbeing could be at risk.

ELKA has a deep-seated belief that she is worthless. As a result, whenever she goes to a party, she drinks huge amounts of alcohol because it makes her feel less inhibited. Typically, she will get so drunk that she injures herself, passes out or vomits. Often she will go off with guys she doesn't know (and isn't interested in or attracted to), because the fact that someone wants to be with her makes her temporarily feel a bit better. The next day, however, she usually feels like she's hit rock bottom. Not only is she hungover, but stories and photos come out about what she did when she was drunk and she feels embarrassed and used. This intensifies her belief that 'There is something seriously wrong with me.'

Reflect

If low self-esteem is an issue for you, how does it influence your behaviours?

THE SELF-FULFILLING PROPHECY

Low self-esteem can become a vicious circle, because our beliefs have a direct effect on our behaviours. If you believe that you are not OK, this will affect the way you behave in the presence of others, which affects the way that they respond back to you. This may in turn reinforce your negative view of yourself.

Because LAUREN feels inadequate, she often withdraws from people and gives out unfriendly vibes. She doesn't look people in the eye, smile or initiate conversation. This makes her appear cold and distant and, as a result, people make little effort to be friendly towards her. Lauren notices that people aren't very friendly to her, so her belief that she is unlikeable is reinforced. It becomes a 'self-fulfilling prophecy' because Lauren's negative beliefs about herself affect her behaviours, which in turn affect the way others treat her.

Lauren's self-fulfilling prophecy

BELIEF: I am not OK.

BEHAVIOUR: Doesn't initiate conversations or look people in the eye.

FEEDBACK: Other people make little effort to be friendly towards me.

PERCEPTION: People don't like me; I am not OK.
(The original belief is reinforced.)

In order to short-circuit this process, we need to become aware of the messages that our behaviour conveys to others, and modify it where possible. (See 'Think about how you communicate', page 115.)

STRATEGIES TO BUILD SELF-ESTEEM

Some people mistakenly think that having high self-esteem means being 'full of yourself' and arrogant — this is not the case at all. People with healthy self-esteem don't need to tell others how great they are because they already feel OK about themselves. In fact, it is often people who have low self-esteem who are inclined to boast or bully others. Putting others down is their way of trying to build themselves up, because they feel inadequate.

There are many benefits associated with healthy self-esteem, such as feeling comfortable in your own skin, having healthy relationships and feeling OK with taking social risks. Of course, high self-esteem is not something we can achieve overnight — it is something that we build over time. Here are some strategies that can help.

PROBLEM-SOLVE

If there is a situation in your life that is affecting your self-esteem, ask yourself: 'What is the best thing I can do to change this situation?' If you are not sure, try using the step-by-step problem-solving strategies outlined in Chapter 11.

OLENA is being bullied by two girls at school, and this is negatively affecting her self-esteem. While she initially did not want to worry her parents, Olena eventually opened up to her mum. Her mum was very concerned and, after a long talk, they came up with various action strategies. First, Olena took screenshots of the abusive comments the girls had posted about her on social media (in case she needed to use it as evidence down the track). Then she blocked their accounts. Next, Olena's mum called the school principal to make her aware of the problem, and to ensure that appropriate action would be taken. In accordance with the school's anti-bullying policy, the

*two girls were dealt with by a senior teacher and put on probation.
Then Olena made regular appointments with the school counsellor to
talk about ways to manage bullying behaviour (such as maintaining
confident body language and not reacting), and to challenge her
own beliefs about being 'not OK'. The counsellor organised a buddy
mentor system with an older student to give her some extra support
at school. She also explained more about reasons for bullying
behaviour (including that some people have a cruel streak, some bully
to bond with others, and some do it because they are insecure and are
trying to make themselves feel superior). Talking to the counsellor
made Olena feel better about herself, and she finally understood that
the girls' bullying behaviour was a reflection of their own issues,
rather than her own inadequacies.*

THINK ABOUT HOW YOU COMMUNICATE

The way we communicate with other people provides information on how
we feel about ourselves. When we tell another person what we think, feel
or want in a clear, assertive way, the unspoken message is: 'I matter. My
opinions and needs are as valid and important as everyone else's.' Assertive
communication encourages other people to treat us respectfully and creates
relationships based on equality (see also Chapter 12 on Communication).

Communication occurs not only in the words we say but also nonverbally
through our manner, body language and tone of voice. When our nonverbal
communication is confident, we convey self-respect. Confident body
language includes an open stance with our shoulders back (not hunched),
our hands resting comfortably (arms not folded defensively in front of us)
and our back straight. We are able to look the other person in the eye, and
speak in a clear and friendly voice (rather than looking down at our shoes and
mumbling). We can use friendly gestures, such as smiling, and asking the
other person how they've been and what they think about particular things.

Our body language and mannerisms say a lot about what is going on
for us internally. Just adopting a self-assured posture and tone can increase
our level of confidence in social situations.

ADDRESS THINKING ERRORS THAT CONTRIBUTE TO POOR SELF-ESTEEM

In Chapter 3, we looked at thinking errors that create unnecessary distress in all sorts of situations. Some types of thinking errors have a direct effect on our self-esteem. These include labelling, overgeneralising, personalising, comparing and 'shoulds'.

LABELLING

When we don't live up to our own expectations, it's easy to label ourselves as 'defective' in some way. You might find yourself using labels like 'idiot', 'failure', 'loser', 'hopeless', 'ugly', 'useless', etc.

Labelling is unreasonable because it is the ultimate overgeneralisation. It is never logical to sum up an entire person based on a specific attribute or event. Each of us is a complex mixture of characteristics, traits, qualities and behaviours, and these can't be encapsulated in one label.

There is a simple antidote to labelling — *be specific*. Whenever you catch yourself using labels, always restate your observations in specific terms. The table below demonstrates some examples.

AVOID LABELLING — BE SPECIFIC

LABEL	SPECIFIC FACTS
I'm dumb.	I'm not very good at physics and chemistry.
I'm such a loser.	I make mistakes at times.
I'm a fat slob.	I'm three kilograms over my ideal weight.
I'm socially incompetent.	I'm shy with people I don't know well.
I'm a failure.	I didn't get the two holiday jobs I applied for.
I failed because I'm dumb.	I failed because I didn't study and maths is not one of my strong subjects.

OVERGENERALISING

When something goes wrong, you might be inclined to overgeneralise about yourself and tell yourself things like: 'I fail at everything that I do', 'Nobody likes me' or 'I always make stupid mistakes'. Overgeneralising is irrational because you make sweeping negative conclusions that go far beyond the current situation. The antidote to overgeneralising is, once again, to be specific — *stick to the facts*. Here are some examples.

AVOID OVERGENERALISING — STICK TO THE FACTS

OVERGENERALISING	SPECIFIC FACTS
I made a complete fool of myself.	I said something that might have sounded silly.
Nobody likes me.	Three girls in my class don't like me.
I'm hopeless at everything I do.	I failed an English test and didn't do as well as I hoped in my history assignment.
I completely screwed up that exam.	I misunderstood one question on the exam.
I wasted the whole day. I achieved nothing!	I got distracted and achieved less than I had planned.

PERSONALISING

When we personalise, we take responsibility for things that are not our fault, or blame ourselves for negative events without taking all the other facts into account. To avoid personalising, you need to *be objective*. The table below contains examples of how to challenge personalising thoughts.

AVOID PERSONALISING — BE OBJECTIVE

PERSONALISING	OBJECTIVE FACTS
They didn't come to my party because they don't like me.	They didn't come to my party because I invited them too late, and they already had other plans.
I don't connect with them — there is something wrong with me.	I don't connect with them — we think differently and have different values.
She felt awkward at my party. It's my fault	She felt awkward at my party. I'm sorry she felt that way (but it is not my fault).

He wasn't very friendly. He obviously doesn't like me.	He wasn't very friendly. He has a cranky personality and was having a particularly bad day.
My parents are getting divorced — it's my fault.	My parents are getting divorced — they have never been able to get along.

COMPARING

If we feel inadequate in some way, we tend to look to other people to see how we compare with them. Many teenagers compare themselves on things like looks, marks, sporting ability, number of friends, clothes, family or even personality.

➤ *ALAN thinks to himself: 'Look how easily Rudi can talk to girls. I can't do that.'*

➤ *RENATE thinks to herself: 'Charlotte's assignment is really good — mine is hopeless.'*

➤ *SAMANTHA thinks to herself: 'Sharon is so confident and outgoing — I'm so quiet compared to her.'*

➤ *SPIRO thinks to himself: 'Jim is really muscly — I'm just a skinny rake.'*

The problem with comparing is that there will always be people who seem to be doing better than we are, so we inevitably end up feeling inadequate. People have different strengths and weaknesses, and focusing on some people's particular strengths creates unrealistic expectations for ourselves. We also don't always know what is really going on in their lives. Sometimes we can be completely wrong about how perfect other people's lives seem.

While it is fine to look to certain individuals for inspiration or as role models, you know you are making unhealthy comparisons when observing other people makes you feel bad about yourself. Instead of comparing yourself, it is better to reflect on and acknowledge your own strengths, have realistic expectations, and set goals that are life-enhancing and relevant for you.

SHOULDS

In Chapter 4, we saw the 'tyranny of the shoulds'. These include beliefs about how we should or shouldn't be, or things that we should or shouldn't do.

The more inflexible our shoulds, the more likely we are to end up feeling inadequate. Rigid expectations of ourselves make us self-critical and dissatisfied.

Shoulds that affect our self-esteem are those that focus on our performance, achievements, appearance and relationships. Below are some examples of shoulds that can contribute to low self-esteem.

PERFORMANCE
'I should always do everything perfectly'
'I should never make mistakes'
'I should always live up to the expectations of my parents and/or teachers'
'I should be good at sport'

ACHIEVEMENTS
'I should get above ninety per cent on all my assessments'
'I should get into the course I want'
'I should always succeed in everything that I try'

APPEARANCE
'I should be thin and attractive'
'I should be tall and muscular'
'I should have nice skin'

RELATIONSHIPS WITH OTHERS
'I should be liked and approved of by lots of people'
'I should have lots of friends'
'I should have an outgoing personality'

Shoulds can make us feel inadequate when we cannot live up to them. Of course, this doesn't mean that we should not try to improve ourselves, or work towards goals. The challenge is to maintain flexibility — that is, to be able to accept ourselves, even when we do not meet all of our expectations. By converting 'shoulds' to 'preferences', we can remain focused on specific goals, but avoid unnecessary distress if we are unable to meet them.

A good way to dispute unhelpful shoulds is to use a statement that includes: 'I prefer ... but ...' This is demonstrated in the following table.

CONVERTING SHOULDS INTO PREFERENCES

SHOULD	PREFERENCE
I should succeed in everything that I attempt.	I prefer to succeed in all my goals and will do the best I can, but sometimes it won't be possible. It is normal and human to not achieve goals at times.
I should have a boyfriend/girlfriend.	I would prefer to have a boyfriend/girlfriend, but I'm OK whether or not that happens.
I should have lots of friends.	I prefer to have lots of friends, but I'm OK, regardless of the number of friends I have.
I should be good at sport.	I would prefer to be good at sport, but I can accept that sport is not my strong suit.
I should always please my parents and/or teachers.	I prefer to please my parents and/or teachers, and much of the time I do. But I'm OK, even if I don't always live up to people's expectations.
I should never make mistakes.	I prefer not to make mistakes, but even if I do sometimes make mistakes, that doesn't mean I'm hopeless, incompetent or dumb.
I should be thin.	I would prefer to be thin, but I accept that I have a stocky build and being thin is unrealistic for me.

DISPUTE UNHELPFUL THINKING USING A STRESS LOG

Whenever you notice that you are feeling bad about yourself, it can be useful to work through a Stress Log. This can serve as a guide for challenging the unhelpful thinking that is contributing to low self-esteem.

ABBY has been struggling with maths for most of the year. She notices that other students in her class seem to grasp the concepts easily and this makes her feel more inadequate. Abby fills in a Stress Log:

ACTIVATING EVENT	Sitting in maths class. Finding it really difficult — I don't get it.
BELIEFS/THOUGHTS Shoulds	I am dumb. I am hopeless. Everyone else can do it, but I can't. I should be able to do this. I should understand maths. If I don't, it means I'm dumb and hopeless.
CONSEQUENCES How did I feel? What did I do?	Inadequate, depressed. Gave up. Sat there and doodled.
DISPUTE Thinking errors Alternative, more balanced view?	Labelling, comparing I am not dumb, but I am not good at maths. This subject has never come naturally to me — I've always found it difficult. I have other strengths, particularly in creative areas. I need to keep working on it to get through it this year, but my maths ability does not reflect who I am as a person.
EFFECTIVE ACTION	Talk to my maths teacher, explain that I'm struggling and ask for some extra help. Ask my friend for help with some specific questions.

EXERCISE: RELEASING THE SELF-CRITICAL BIAS

Our beliefs influence the way we think and how we direct our attention. Once we believe something, we keep noticing things that confirm those beliefs, and ignoring things that disprove them. This is called a *bias* in our thinking. If you have low self-esteem, you are more likely to notice and recall things that confirm your negative view of yourself, and to ignore or forget experiences that don't fit in with that view.

To overcome the negative bias, it can be helpful to think about positive, affirming experiences from your past. These might be times when you were successful, when you connected with others, when you felt like you belonged, when you felt totally comfortable with the person you are or when you felt proud of yourself. Once you can remember some examples, you can learn strategies to keep these positive experiences at the front of your mind.

The following exercise will help you to focus on memories of positive experiences, and therefore reverse the bias towards negative perceptions. It is best to spend a couple of hours to work through the first three steps, as the more details you can come up with, the more effective the exercise will be.

Exercise

1   Write down five events from your past that *made you feel good about yourself* at the time. For example, you may have felt proud for achieving something important, felt special to someone or felt liked and accepted in a group.

Although you may initially say that nothing comes to mind, most people find that if they take the time to think about it, they can usually come up with a number of such past events. (If you are feeling stuck, talking to a family member or someone who knows you well may help you to come up with examples.)

2   Write down a detailed description of each of those five events. This part of the exercise is the most time-consuming, but it is worth the time and effort (and most people actually enjoy writing about positive, affirming situations from their past). To help with visualising later, try to note down as many details as you can about each event. For example, what were you wearing? What was the weather like that day? Can you recall any particular smells or sounds?

3   After you have described each of those five memories in detail, give each one a simple title. For example:
    a. 'Lots of praise from my rowing team'
    b. 'Speech Night performance two years ago'
    c. 'Tony said I'm the best friend he's ever had'
    d. 'Walking home from school with Ingrid and her brother'
    e. 'Stuart asked me to join their team for the inter-school coding challenge'
Write the titles of your own five events in the space below.
    a.
    b.
    c.
    d.
    e.

4   The next task might sound a little strange, but it is actually a very powerful way to reinforce memories that you want to repeatedly bring to mind. It

is called *method of loci*, and involves connecting each memory with a specific location that you pass daily (or regularly).

Visualise the route that you take each day as you go to and from school (or work, or other locations you visit frequently). Picture any landmarks that you pass along your way. Now briefly describe five of those landmarks. For example:

a. Park with cannons
b. Thai takeaway shop
c. Post office
d. Massive gum tree
e. House with the barking dog

Five landmarks that I pass:

a.
b.
c.
d.
e.

5 Now here comes the most interesting, creative part! Visualise the first landmark on your list and, using your imagination, connect that landmark to one of the memories that you listed in step 3. The way that you connect the two things doesn't need to be realistic. In fact, it can be ridiculous or bizarre. You just need to create some sort of connection between the memory and the landmark that you often pass.

For example:

- You might visualise the park with the cannons and see yourself doing your speech night presentation in front of the cannons.
- You might visualise the post office and imagine your rowing team going inside to register for the Olympic Games.
- You might visualise the massive gum tree, and see Tony sitting under it, saying that you are his best friend ever.
- You might visualise Ingrid and her brother, with whom you had fond memories of walking home from school, eating Thai food at the takeaway shop.
- You might visualise the house with the barking dog and see your coding team working on computers with the dog sitting happily beside them.

Notice that there doesn't need to be any logical connection between each memory and the landmark you match it with. Even if they are totally weird, your mind will be prompted to make the connection whenever you pass the landmark. If you pass these locations on a regular basis, these memories will get lots of reinforcement.

Although it may seem a bit bizarre, this exercise can have a profound effect on the content of your thoughts. By prompting you to remember events that you would normally ignore, it can undo the negative thinking bias that typically accompanies low self-esteem. It can also provide a fascinating insight into how our mind works!

STRENGTHS RECORD

Another exercise that can help reverse the cognitive bias is keeping a record of your personal strengths, together with evidence that demonstrates each one. Start by identifying at least five strengths or positive qualities that you have. Then, for each one, think of two recent examples of times that you demonstrated that quality. They don't have to be anything huge — even acknowledging the smallest things can be helpful.

Example: EVA'S list

Strength/Positive Quality: PERSISTENT

1. *Finished the hike on our school camp (even though I was completely shattered!).*
2. *Even though I find English hard, I put in a huge effort this term and managed to pass the exam.*

Strength/Positive Quality: THOUGHTFUL

1. *I texted Mum on the way to her job interview to wish her good luck — I knew how nervous she was feeling.*
2. *Lou loved the blue necklace I gave her for her birthday — I picked it because I remembered her favourite colour is blue.*

Strength/Positive Quality: FUNNY

1. *Everyone was laughing when I told them my 'dog' story the other day.*
2. *Danielle says hearing my hysterical giggles always makes her laugh (in a good way).*

Strength/Positive Quality: PHYSICALLY STRONG

1. *I have been sticking to my exercise plan and am feeling much fitter.*
2. *I was able to paddle all the way out the back on my surfboard yesterday, even though the waves were big and the rips were strong.*

Strength/Positive Quality: KIND

1. *When I saw a toddler fall off his scooter the other day, my instinct was to run over and help him. He seemed comforted by me.*
2. *I ring Grandma every week to say 'hi' and see how she is going. She says it is one of the highlights of her week and she loves having a chat.*

If you are feeling stuck doing this exercise, ask yourself: What qualities do I like about myself or feel good about? What positive characteristics have other people commented on? Here are some possible ideas: good listener, creative, fun, adventurous, supportive, friendly, welcoming to others, great hair, nice eyes, appreciative, passionate, loyal, committed, ethical, determined to make a difference, calm, patient, enthusiastic, particular talent(s), eye for detail, approachable, reliable, good friend ... Write your responses on the form below.

Strength/Positive Quality:
Examples of times when this quality was demonstrated:
1.
2.

Strength/Positive Quality:
Examples:
1.
2.

Strength/Positive Quality:
Examples:
1.
2.

Strength/Positive Quality:
Examples:
1.
2.

Strength/Positive Quality:
Examples:
1.
2.

An alternative approach is to keep a record of your strengths and examples on your phone or computer; you can include images as well. Over time, whenever you think of other examples, be sure to add them.

PRACTISE SELF-ACCEPTANCE

Most of us have things we don't like about ourselves. Some of these may be within our control (to some degree), but others are not. Having traits we don't particularly like does not in itself diminish our self-esteem. The problem is the *inability to accept those traits* as being part of who we are.

You might not be as funny, as tall, as smart, as popular, as successful, as attractive, or as admired as other people you know, or as you would like to be. In fact, you may never be the way you would ideally like. However, focusing on your shortcomings and insisting that you should not be this way will not change who you are, and it will just make you feel inadequate. Is there any point?

The challenge is to try to change the things that matter, if they are within our control, and accept the things that we cannot change. Acceptance means *relaxing into the reality of the way things are*, and giving up the struggle against things we can't do anything about.

To use a simple example, instead of wondering 'Does my bum look big in this?' when you are out at a social function, forget about your bum and focus on the conversation you are having. You may never be happy with your bum, but when you stop focusing on it and just accept it, it stops being an issue. You can enjoy the social function without worrying about it.

Self-acceptance means learning to be comfortable with every facet of who we are — including our perceived imperfections. When we truly accept something, it stops being a sore point. We can relax and feel satisfied with ourselves.

SET LIFE-ENHANCING GOALS

While there are some things we need to accept about ourselves, there may be other things we can change or improve. For things that are within our control, it might be useful to set goals and work towards making positive changes. (See also Chapter 13 on Setting Goals.)

For example:

➤ If you feel not OK because people often take advantage of you, it might be useful to learn assertive communication skills.

➤ If you feel not OK because you have difficulty with some of your school work, it might be useful to get some help and improve your study habits.

➤ If you feel not OK because you are very unfit, it might be useful to work on building up your fitness.

➤ If you are feeling not OK in some social situations, it might be useful to work on conversation skills and on taking more social risks.

Of course, the goals you choose to set for yourself will depend on the issues that are of particular concern to you. Think about what sort of things might help you feel better about yourself, and whether there is anything you can do to achieve them.

If you do decide to work towards particular goals, make sure you maintain a *flexible attitude*. This means accepting yourself whether or not you achieve your goals. Avoid *conditional* self-acceptance (e.g. 'I will be OK if I can pass that exam/lose three kilograms/make some new friends', etc.). Being flexible means telling yourself: 'I'd like to and I'll do my best, but I'm OK regardless of whether or not I succeed.'

BEING DIFFERENT

While the desire to belong to a 'tribe' is normal for all human beings, it feels particularly important during our teenage years. For this reason, some teens try to suppress parts of themselves, or go along with behaviours they are not comfortable with, in an attempt to make themselves more likeable. The trouble is that trying to be someone you are not usually doesn't work. It may not feel right to you and may come across as inauthentic or fake. (And even if some people like the persona you put on, it never feels as if they like the real you.)

> *TAYA has always been shy by nature. She often feels nervous when interacting with people she doesn't know, and in social situations she prefers to listen and chip in occasionally, rather than be the centre of attention. Many of Taya's friends, however, are outgoing and have lots to say. In the past, Taya has tried to be extroverted like them but it has never worked or felt right. Taya is learning to accept that she is shy by nature. Between thirty and forty per cent of the population are introverted by inclination, so she is by no means alone. While Taya works to get over her shyness by initiating social contact with some of her friends, and going to social events when opportunities come up, she also accepts that her personality style is different to her outgoing friends. Interestingly, when she stops trying to imitate them, she feels more comfortable with herself and feels accepted by them as well.*

'Always be a first-rate version of yourself,
and not a second-rate version of someone else.'
JUDY GARLAND

You might notice that people who have good self-esteem are authentic — they don't try to be someone they are not, even if they are quite different from others. Unless their behaviour is offensive (that is, rude or insensitive to others), the fact that they are different is usually not a problem. It is the self-criticism and negative judgement about being different that usually impairs self-esteem. The reality is you can't please everyone and some people may not like you, no matter how hard you try. Accepting your own personal quirks and differences, and acknowledging they are part of who you are, is usually the best way to go and is a sign of healthy self-esteem.

PETER is passionate about astronomy and often talks excitedly about the planets. Recently, he has been teased by some of the boys in his class and he now feels bad about himself. Peter fills in a Stress Log as follows:

ACTIVATING EVENT	I was talking about astronomy, and some of the boys were laughing at me and calling me a 'dork'.
BELIEFS/THOUGHTS	They don't like me. I don't fit in. I'm a loser. If other guys my age don't share my interests, it means there is something wrong with me.
Shoulds	I should be like everyone else. I should fit in.
CONSEQUENCES How did I feel? What did I do?	Embarrassed, sad, inadequate. Ignored them.
DISPUTE Thinking errors	Personalising, labelling I'm different from many of the boys in my class, but that doesn't mean there's something wrong with me. It's OK to be different, and to have different interests and ways of thinking.
Alternative, more balanced view?	Some people are narrow-minded and behave stupidly. They judge people on random things, rather than on who they really are. I don't have to live up to their expectations. I prefer to be liked, but I can cope if some kids don't like me.
EFFECTIVE ACTION	Focus on the friendships I already have and enjoy what I'm interested in. Look into joining an astronomy group where I can meet people who are as passionate about planets as I am. Don't try to please everyone.

While Peter went through a rough patch during Year 11, over time, many students ended up liking and respecting him. Peter knew he was different to other boys in his class, but he resisted the temptation to try to be like them. While he listened to what others had to say, he didn't pretend he always agreed with them and he usually spoke his mind honestly. He also continued to focus on the things that interested him. Eventually, Peter met other boys with similar interests and his final year at school, as well as his university years, were much happier for him.

There is an important lesson for all of us here:

JUST BECAUSE YOU DON'T FIT IN, DOESN'T MEAN THERE IS SOMETHING WRONG WITH YOU.

Many people who end up happy and successful in their adult lives have felt alone and different during their high-school years. If you do an online search for 'happy and successful people who didn't fit in at school', you will find examples of people from all walks of life, including prime ministers, scientists, famous actors and authors. Social pressures that happen during adolescence lead many teens to use superficial benchmarks to promote themselves and evaluate others (such as clothes, haircuts, looks, hanging out with certain people and acting 'cool'). Things that people come to value more as adults (such as having a good moral compass; having an interest in ideas; and being genuine, accepting, respectful and caring towards others) may not rate highly for many adolescents. As we get older, our attitudes and behaviour towards others changes. Many teens who experience their school years as lonely or miserable grow up to find friendships, happiness and meaning later in their lives.

IN A NUTSHELL ...

➤ Our self-esteem is the way we perceive our own worth. Healthy self-esteem enables us to enjoy social relationships and feel comfortable within ourselves.

➤ If we feel 'not OK' in ourselves, the way we behave may give negative messages to others, which may serve to maintain low self-esteem. This is called the 'self-fulfilling prophecy'.

➤ There are a number of strategies we can use to improve self-esteem, including challenging the thinking that perpetuates low self-esteem, practising self-acceptance, setting life-enhancing goals, addressing the cognitive bias towards self-criticism and recognising that it's OK to be different.

TEN

Mindfulness

Mindfulness is a form of self-awareness training that has been adapted from traditional Buddhist practices, cultivated over thousands of years. In the last few decades, people in Western countries have started understanding the helpful role it can play in reducing stress, managing emotions and preventing mental-health problems. There has been a lot of talk about mindfulness on TV and radio, in books, online and also in many schools, so you may have already heard about it. But what exactly *is* mindfulness, and how does it work?

Mindfulness is a way of using your mind so that you are totally connected to what is happening in the present moment. Normally, our mind is full of thoughts about all sorts of things, including issues from the past and what might happen in the future. During a state of mindfulness, we focus on experiencing things as they are happening right now. We become more aware of what is going on inside ourselves (including thoughts, feelings, body sensations or tastes), as well as things happening in our external environment (like sounds and smells). We learn not to judge our experience, even those parts that are unpleasant or uncomfortable. By being fully present, we can appreciate some of the good things that we might otherwise miss when our mind is wandering. It also helps us experience unwanted events in a more open and accepting way.

Mindfulness can be practised through meditation, or through making a deliberate effort to pay attention to things happening in the present moment.

MINDFULNESS MEDITATION

In mindfulness meditation, the idea is to focus our attention on a simple object or thing and use this to 'anchor' our mind, so that we can remain focused on the present. With time, this process helps to quieten the mind, so that it is no longer racing from one thought to another. It is a bit like a snow globe — our scattered thoughts are like the snow after the globe has been shaken, but mindfulness helps the 'snow' to settle. Our mind learns to be more still.

Many things can be used as point of focus when practising mindfulness meditation. The most common is the breath, but you can also use sounds or the sensations in your body as you move. Whenever we notice that our thoughts have wandered from our point of focus, we gently bring our attention back to it. If you are using your breath as your point of focus, pay attention to the breath in its own natural rhythm. (This is different to the *slow rhythmic breathing* exercise described in Chapter 7, because in meditation you are not trying to change or control anything — you are just observing.)

Ideally, meditation is practised every day (or most days) in a quiet place, sitting upright on a chair, stool or pillow. The best time to do it is when you are alert, and not in a hurry to do anything or be anywhere else. Trying to meditate when you are tired is not a good idea, as you are likely to fall asleep, and sleep is not the same as meditation.

When you first start to practise meditation, chances are you will find it quite challenging, as your mind will keep 'pulling' towards thoughts. Sometimes your thoughts might be racing and your mind will dart from one topic to another at high speed. This is particularly likely if you feel stressed or emotionally stirred up. At times, you will get so caught up in thoughts that you will forget about meditating. This is completely normal. Try not to judge your performance. Accept that your mind will wander, and once you notice it, simply acknowledge, 'This is a thought,' and gently bring your attention back to your point of focus.

Focusing on a single thing for more than a few seconds is usually tricky to begin with, because we are not used to it and our mind is in the habit of choosing its own thoughts. It does, however, get easier with practice. For this reason, you might initially choose to meditate for just a few minutes per session and gradually increase the amount of time. Some people say that twenty-minute sessions are ideal, although it might be helpful to occasionally do longer ones.

WHY MEDITATE?

Given that meditation can be challenging, and that it may feel like there are many more interesting things to do with your time, you may be thinking, 'Why put myself through it on a regular basis?' There are lots of benefits. Probably the most common reason people choose to meditate is to manage emotions. Regular practice helps to reduce the intensity of upsetting emotions (such as anxiety, frustration, anger and sadness), and may prevent the development of more troubling mental-health issues. For people who have experienced bouts of depression, mindfulness practice may help to prevent further episodes.

Mindfulness also helps us to use our mind in a more focused way. This can be beneficial for anything that requires concentration, such as reading, studying, solving a maths problem or staying focused when someone is talking. It means that our mind is not cluttered with lots of thoughts when we are trying to pay attention.

EXERCISE: ONE-MINUTE FOCUS ON YOUR BREATH
Set the timer on your phone to one minute. Sit upright in your chair, close your eyes and pay attention to your breathing for the full minute. Have a go — try it now.

Although it sounds straightforward, many people who do this exercise initially find it difficult. They become aware of how busy their minds really are and how hard it is to focus on something simple like your breath, even for one minute. If you practise this exercise on a daily basis, you will find it becomes much easier and, over time, you will probably be able to meditate for fifteen to twenty minutes or more.

Once you learn this technique, you can practise mini meditation sessions at any time, such as when you are going for a walk, sitting in class before a lesson has begun, travelling on public transport or about to do an exam. Even a few minutes of meditation can have a calming effect.

LEARNING TO MEDITATE

While some people can teach themselves to meditate, others prefer to learn with the help of external guidance. You might consider signing up for a class, or using guided spoken instructions found online. There are also some free apps, containing guided mindfulness exercises, available for download. Two popular apps that are available for free are: *Smiling Mind*: smilingmind.com.au and *Giant Mind*: www.1giantmind.org.

EXERCISE: MINDFUL AWARENESS OF THE PRESENT MOMENT

Sit upright in your chair, close your eyes and then ask yourself this question: 'What is going on for me right now?' What do you notice?

Become aware of what is happening for you in this moment. How are you feeling, right now? Good? Bad? Neutral? Are there any issues or concerns that you are carrying in the back of your mind? If so, notice their presence.

Is there any uneasiness or anxiety going on for you right now? If so, where in your body do you feel it? Perhaps you are aware of some 'back of the mind' thoughts that connect with those feelings?

Notice the physical sensations you are experiencing right now — the point of contact between your body in the chair, the weight of your arms and legs, the sensations of your clothes touching your skin, your feet inside your shoes, your hair touching your scalp.

Notice any thoughts that pop into your mind. If you become aware that you are having a thought, just acknowledge it: 'Ah, that's a thought.'

Notice the sounds that you can hear, including sounds coming from inside the room and sounds coming from outside.

Whatever you notice, observe it with a completely open and accepting mind. No trying, no striving. It is as if you are an external observer of your own experience, witnessing all the details without judging anything.

After a few minutes, you can open your eyes. You might like to jot down what you noticed.

AKIRA has been feeling very stressed for the past few weeks. She has been super busy working on a major art project but, now that it has been submitted, she still feels on edge. Akira has organised a gathering at her place on the weekend but, instead of feeling excited about it, she feels apprehensive. What's going on?

Akira decides to take some time out to sit on the beanbag in her room and mindfully tune in to what is happening for her right now. She notices that her breathing is quite fast and there are butterflies in her tummy. She also becomes aware that she is feeling anxious and a bit flat. Akira allows herself to view these feelings with curiosity, like an outside observer, without trying to change them. Now she notices lots of thoughts darting around in her mind. Many relate to her artwork: 'I chose the wrong medium — I should have stuck with the original version … It was such a waste of time … So much work, and the final product was rubbish.' Other thoughts are about her gathering: 'Maybe no one will come … Will my different friends mix? … Will they get bored? … I hope Dad doesn't embarrass me …' Now she turns her attention to the natural rhythm of her breath. As the different thoughts keep popping into her mind, Akira acknowledges that she is having thoughts, and returns her attention to her breath. Thoughts come and go, and Akira keeps returning to her breath. After twenty minutes, Akira notices she is feeling a lot calmer. Her objective situation hasn't changed but Akira feels like things are really not so bad. As her anxiety has dropped, Akira is able to think in a more reasonable and balanced way.

MINDFUL AWARENESS IN DAILY LIFE

In addition to meditation, mindfulness can also be practised in our daily life situations. This involves becoming more present and aware of what we are experiencing in the moment. For example, you might focus on the sensations of the food you are eating (smells, textures, flavours). Or, when you take a shower, you might home in on the sensations of the warmth and pressure of the water on your skin, and the sounds you can hear, both inside and outside of the shower. You can be mindful as you walk, by focusing on simple things such as your breath; the physical sensations of each foot as it touches the ground; the feeling of the sun or wind on your skin; or the sounds of birds, traffic and voices in the distance. Your ability to practise mindful awareness in daily-life situations will be improved by practising mindfulness meditation regularly.

> **EXERCISE: MINDFUL EATING**
>
> Instead of our usual habit of eating while checking out social media, reading, listening to music or watching TV, mindful eating involves being totally present with our current experience of eating. Pay full attention to the sensation of every piece of food that you put in your mouth. Notice how it looks, how it smells, how it feels and, finally, how it tastes, as you chew it slowly. Notice the jaw muscles that you are using to chew and the way the inside of your mouth contracts when you swallow. Close your eyes to experience the sensations more fully. Many people who do this are amazed at how rich and interesting the process of eating really is — something that we take for granted most of the time!

WITHOUT JUDGEMENT

Mindfulness involves accepting whatever we notice in this moment, without judging it in any way. For example, if we are experiencing emotions such as sadness, anger, anxiety, guilt or frustration, we observe every aspect of those emotions with curiosity and openness. If we are hearing unpleasant sounds, such as traffic, sirens or loud machinery, we relax into those sounds without trying to resist them or block them out. If we are experiencing uncomfortable body sensations, such as tension related to stress or pain related to injury, we notice what these sensations feel like (for instance, tight, achy or hot) with acceptance. We sit with the discomfort, without struggling against it. We let it be. Is this different from the way you would normally react when something is not right with you?

Not judging our experiences might seem difficult. We are always judging things and sometimes it can even be enjoyable. Why wouldn't you want to judge? The answer is that negative judgements add an extra level of suffering to our lives. Not only are we dealing with the original problem (e.g. pain, noise, sadness) but, by judging it, we are creating a second problem for ourselves — upsetting emotions (e.g. frustration, anger or despair). Two problems for the price of one!

When we judge our anxiety or depression as being a really bad thing, and something we must eliminate at all costs, it becomes 'the enemy'. The more we hate it, the more of a threat it becomes, and the more it grows. We can end up with anxiety about our anxiety, or depression about our depression! Strangely enough, when we sit with unpleasant emotions or experiences and observe their qualities without resisting or trying to make them go away, the experience itself becomes less upsetting to us. Instead of the tension and distress that comes with trying to push it away, we can allow ourselves to experience it more fully. We relax into it. If we can learn to accept unpleasant sensations or experiences, any extra suffering that comes with them may be reduced, or may even disappear altogether. Buddhist philosophy says that suffering actually comes from the expectation that we should not suffer. Becoming upset about unpleasant events or experiences only adds to our suffering.

Not judging unpleasant experiences does not mean that we stop caring about things. It is helpful and appropriate to set goals, and to work on improving aspects of our lives that we are able to change. However, releasing judgement during mindfulness practice can teach us another way of responding to things that we can't control. It is also helpful to remember that unpleasant emotions are normal and we don't need to always push them away. As we saw in Chapter 1, emotions such as anger, sadness, anxiety or resentment can sometimes be helpful, because they motivate us to problem-solve, or take action to address particular challenges. A mindful attitude can enable us to tolerate upsetting emotions without getting too stressed about them. With time, the emotions will pass all by themselves.

NOTICING YOUR OWN THOUGHT PATTERNS

One of the other benefits of mindfulness is that it gives us greater insight into our own thought processes. Concentrating on something simple, like our breath, sounds or body sensations, provides a 'platform' from which we can observe our own thoughts. It gives us something to return to when we realise that our mind has wandered. It also helps us to become more aware of where our mind is wandering to.

As you become more skilled at paying attention, it becomes easier to identify unhelpful thinking habits such as worrying, overthinking and ruminating. For instance, you might notice how your mind gets caught up in thoughts created by anxiety, such as 'what ifs', overanalysing and overthinking. Mindful observation might help you notice that these thoughts generate more anxiety, which in turn creates more unhelpful thoughts and keeps the cycle going. You might also become aware of how often your mind goes over everything you need to do. Busy people often carry a vague 'to-do list' in the back of their mind. It may feel like you need to do this so that you won't forget anything, but in reality it takes up a lot of attention and mental space that could be used for more important things (such as focusing on what your teacher is saying). Instead of a mental checklist, why not keep a written list that you can refer to? Writing things down, and crossing them off the list once they have been completed, is a more effective way of staying on top of the things you need to do. It also frees your mind to concentrate on whatever requires your attention right now.

By observing what's going on in our own minds, we can start to identify unhelpful thinking habits and begin to disconnect from them. Labelling unhelpful thinking as we catch ourselves doing it (for example, 'I am overthinking this again', 'Oh, that's rumination', or 'That's another worry thought') reminds us that they are just thoughts, and not necessarily reality. Thoughts can be helpful or unhelpful, true or untrue, and biased or reasonable. Next time you are overthinking, overanalysing, worrying or ruminating, try to *catch yourself in the act* and return your attention to whatever is happening in your present moment. Doing this repeatedly will strengthen your mindfulness skills, improve your ability to disconnect from unhelpful thinking habits, and improve your mood and emotions over time.

Of course, it will not always be possible to keep your mind focused on the present moment. When your emotions are particularly intense, your thoughts will be powerful and intrusive — they will just keep popping into your mind. It may feel like they have a life of their own and there is nothing you can do to manage them. In these situations, the best thing to do is observe what your mind is doing and the way thoughts keep entering your mind. Acknowledge that these thoughts are being triggered by intense emotions, and let them be. Although the thoughts might be unpleasant, they, and the emotions connected to them, will not last forever. With time, they will become less intense, and eventually they will disappear.

Reflect:

How could you incorporate mindfulness meditation into your daily life? Are there times that you could set aside for regular practice? What would you need to prepare?

Are there regular activities that you could link with practising mindful awareness in daily life? (e.g. When you take a shower, walk the dog, eat your breakfast or wait at the bus stop?)

Are there any prompts you could use to remind yourself to switch off 'auto pilot' for a few minutes each day and bring your awareness to the present moment? (e.g. A quote or picture on your screensaver, an alert on your phone or a bookmark in your diary?)

WHAT OTHERS SAY ABOUT MINDFULNESS:

'Mindfulness is simply being aware of what is happening right now without wishing it were different; enjoying the pleasant without holding on when it changes (which it will); being with the unpleasant without fearing it will always be this way (which it won't).'

JAMES BARAZ
AWAKENING JOY FOR KIDS

'Feel the feeling but don't become the emotion.
Witness it. Allow it. Release it.'

CRYSTAL ANDRUS MORISSETTE
THE EMOTIONAL EDGE

'The best way to capture moments is to pay attention.
This is how we cultivate Mindfulness.'

JON KAHAT-ZINN
WHEREVER YOU GO, THERE YOU ARE: MINDFULNESS MEDITATION IN EVERYDAY LIFE

'Mindfulness isn't difficult. We just need to remember to do it.'

SHARON SALZBERG
REAL HAPPINESS: THE POWER OF MEDITATION

'Do not dwell on the past, Do not dream of the future,
Concentrate the mind on the present moment.'

BUDDHA
SOURCE UNKNOWN, THOUGH OFTEN ATTRIBUTED TO *SIDDHARTA BUDDHA, 563–483 BC*

IN A NUTSHELL ...

➤ Mindfulness is a way of using our mind so that we are connected to what is happening in the present moment.

➤ It can be practised as meditation or as heightened awareness in our daily-life situations.

➤ Mindfulness can help to reduce the intensity of upsetting emotions, improve our ability to focus and increase our awareness of what is happening within our own mind.

➤ Learning not to judge our current experience is a key aspect of mindfulness practice.

ELEVEN

Problem-solving

Problems are a normal part of life. Although not all problems are easy to resolve, when we think of them as a puzzle to be worked out, we are more likely to find solutions. Our attitude to dealing with problems is important, because it affects whether or not we become frustrated, anxious, despondent or depressed when we face them. It affects our willingness to explore options, confront challenges and persevere when the going gets tough. In some cases, the solutions to problems are obvious, and we just need to act on them. In other situations, there are no clear solutions and we need to consider various options before we can decide on the best way forward.

> *CONNIE had been excited all week about going to a concert with her friend Cath on Friday night. She was in the middle of getting ready when the phone rang — it was Cath saying that she couldn't make it, because she had to stay home to babysit her younger sister. Connie was shattered: 'I can't believe she's cancelled at the last minute — I've been looking forward to this night for ages. This is just the worst!' So Connie sat at home on Friday night, feeling very angry and upset. Hanging around, overthinking and overanalysing what had happened made her feel even worse.*

How do you think Connie would have felt if, instead of dwelling on the problem, she tried to find solutions? When we do something towards solving a problem, we feel more in charge and are more likely to get our needs met. If Connie had taken the time to think about other options, she might have come up with the following possible solutions:

➤ Calling some other friends and asking if they were free to come along
➤ Asking her brother to come to the concert with her
➤ Going to the concert by herself
➤ Downloading a good movie and watching it as 'compensation' entertainment

STEP-BY-STEP PROBLEM-SOLVING

For problems that have no obvious answers, it can be useful to use step-by-step problem-solving. This is a creative process, where you consider lots of possible options and finally identify which of those options are likely to be the most helpful. While not every situation can be resolved, and you may not always get the exact outcome you would like, it feels good to know that you have done what you can to find solutions.

The step-by-step problem-solving approach involves eight steps:

STEP 1: DEFINE THE PROBLEM

When you are defining a problem, it is important to be specific. Sometimes you will find several problems tied in together. In these situations, try to separate out each component so you can work on each one individually. For example, 'I hate my school' can be broken down to:

➤ 'Some of my classmates make fun of me, which makes me feel bad.'
➤ 'I get upset when Mr Simpson picks on me.'
➤ 'I feel exhausted because I don't get enough time out from studying.'

These are three distinct issues, which, although related, are best dealt with one at a time.

STEP 2: WORK OUT YOUR GOALS FOR THIS PROBLEM

Identify specific outcomes that you would like to achieve and make sure that they are within your control. So, for example, 'All the mean people in my class will disappear' might be a wish, but it is not a realistic goal. However, 'I will spend more time with people I like, such as Emmy and Jo' is a reasonable goal, because it is something you can control. Similarly, hoping 'Mr Simpson will leave' is unrealistic, while 'Work out a strategy to help me cope with Mr Simpson' is reasonable.

STEP 3: BRAINSTORM POSSIBLE SOLUTIONS TO THE PROBLEM

Ask yourself: 'What are some possible things I could do to help resolve this problem?' and be creative! Come up with as many possible solutions as you can. Some of your ideas may be 'out there' — but at this stage you are not evaluating how 'good' or 'bad' they are. For example, some of the possible ways of dealing with annoying people in your class might be to:

➤ Totally ignore them
➤ Be rude back to them
➤ Be nice to them, regardless of how they speak to me
➤ Talk to one or two of them and tell them how I feel
➤ Change schools
➤ Tell my year coordinator or school counsellor, and ask to change classes
➤ Hit them over their heads with a hard object
➤ Ask my parents to contact the parents of the main culprits

Remember to think creatively and don't pass any judgement (for now). Try it — it can be fun!

STEP 4: RULE OUT IMPRACTICAL OR UNREALISTIC OPTIONS

Go through your ideas list and cross out any that are unrealistic or obviously unhelpful. For example, 'Hit them over their heads' might be struck off at this stage.

STEP 5: IDENTIFY THE 'PROS' AND 'CONS' OF THE REMAINING OPTIONS

Now go through the options that are left, and write down the pros and cons of each. For example, being rude back to your classmates might help you let off steam (pro), but it might also make the situation escalate further (con). Being nice to them in spite of their put-downs may make you feel frustrated (con), but it might positively change the way some of them respond to you (pro). Explaining to the others that you don't like the way they are treating you might make you feel embarrassed (con), but at least they will know how you feel (pro).

STEP 6: IDENTIFY YOUR BEST OPTIONS

Once you've considered the pros and cons for each possible solution, it's time to make a decision. Go through the options and pick out the ones that are the most practical and potentially helpful. There may be one really good option that stands out from the others. Or, if there are a few possible solutions, you might be able to put all of them into practice. For instance, with the above example, you may decide to talk to the people who are hassling you and explain how you feel and what you want. If it continues happening, you may then decide to go to the year coordinator to discuss the problem and ask to change classes.

STEP 7: IMPLEMENT THE BEST OPTIONS

Now it's time to make a plan and act on your solutions. For example, you might approach one of the girls in your class who makes nasty comments, and use an 'I-statement' to tell her how you feel and what you would like (see 'Use I-Statements' page 166). You might even write down beforehand what you intend to say, so that you have it clear in your mind. If this doesn't work, your next action might be to talk to the year coordinator or school counsellor about your concerns.

STEP 8: EVALUATE THE RESULTS

The last step is to review how things went when you tried to implement your solutions. What happened? Did it change the situation or do you need to try another approach? If your current strategy worked, that's great. If it didn't, consider going back to your list of options and exploring other strategies.

RECAP: THE STEP-BY-STEP PROBLEM-SOLVING APPROACH

Step 1: Define the problem (be specific).

Step 2: Work out your goals for this problem (be realistic).

Step 3: Brainstorm possible solutions to the problem (don't judge them yet).

Step 4: Rule out impractical or unrealistic options.

Step 5: Identify the 'pros' and 'cons' of the remaining options.

Step 6: Identify your best options.

Step 7: Implement the best options.

Step 8: Evaluate the results.

STEP-BY-STEP PROBLEM-SOLVING IN ACTION

TREVOR has an important assessment coming up, which involves giving a ten-minute speech in front of his class. Trevor hates public speaking and has always managed to find ways to get out of it. This time, however, he can't avoid it because it's part of his assessment. Trevor feels terrified. He decides to use the step-by-step problem-solving approach to help him work out what to do.

STEP 1: DEFINE THE PROBLEM (BE SPECIFIC)

I have to give a talk in my English class next week and I don't want to do it because I'm terrified.

STEP 2: WORK OUT YOUR GOALS FOR THIS PROBLEM (BE REALISTIC)

To be able to get up and give the talk in front of the class.

STEP 3: BRAINSTORM POSSIBLE SOLUTIONS TO THE PROBLEM (DON'T JUDGE THEM YET)

➤ Don't think about it — just get up and do it on the day.

➤ Record my speech and listen to it over and over again.

➤ Write my speech out and practise it in front of Mum and Dad.

➤ Do some research and ask people about ways to give a good presentation.

➤ Use some relaxation strategies to help me stay calm.

➤ Pretend to be sick on the day of the talk so I can get out of doing it.

STEP 4: RULE OUT IMPRACTICAL OR UNREALISTIC OPTIONS

➤ ~~Don't think about it — just get up and do it on the day~~. (This won't work because I actually need to prepare something.)

➤ Record my speech and listen to it over and over again.

➤ Write my speech out and practise it in front of Mum and Dad.

➤ Do some research and ask people about ways to give a good presentation.

➤ Use some relaxation strategies to help me stay calm.

➤ ~~Pretend to be sick on the day of the talk so I can get out of doing it~~. (Even if I miss one day, they will make me do it when I'm back at school.)

STEP 5: IDENTIFY THE 'PROS' AND 'CONS' OF YOUR REMAINING OPTIONS

1. Record my speech and listen to it over and over again.

   Pros: I will know my material well and be familiar with what to say and how to present it. I'll be less likely to go blank if I get nervous.
   Cons: Takes time and effort. I get embarrassed listening to myself.

2. Write my speech and practise it in front of Mum and Dad.

   Pros: Would be good to get used to speaking in front of a live audience.

Cons: It will be hard for me to take it seriously — I might end up laughing.

3. Do some research and ask people about ways to give a good presentation.

Pros: Will get some useful hints, which would probably help my confidence.

Cons: Would take some effort and running around to find people with speaking experience.

4. Use some relaxation strategies to help me stay calm.

Pros: Would help me to relax, and maybe also help in other situations when I feel stressed.

Cons: Would need to find information and some audio of relaxation exercises, so that I know what to do. Relaxation takes time and effort.

6. IDENTIFY YOUR BEST OPTIONS

I am going to write my speech over the next two days. Then I'm going to:

1. Record my speech and listen to it over and over.
2. Practise it in front of Mum and Dad.
3. Use some relaxation strategies.

7. IMPLEMENT THE BEST OPTIONS

I've written my speech, recorded it and listened to it a few times. I've done my speech in front of Mum — she thought it was good. I will do it again for Dad. I have also been listening to a relaxation exercise I downloaded, and I'm learning how to control my breathing. It makes me feel calmer and it's something I can use when I get nervous.

8. EVALUATE THE RESULTS

I did all of the things I had planned and practised the speech a lot before I gave my talk. I still got pretty nervous and forgot to say a couple of things, but I think it went OK. The good thing is I got through it! (See 'Step-by-step problem-solving guide' at the end of this chapter.)

DEVELOP COPING STRATEGIES

Although problem-solving often helps us to find solutions, some situations are not fixable, in spite of our best efforts. If you have tried various strategies and none have worked, it may be time to focus on coping strategies. These are thoughts and actions you can take to help you manage your emotions in situations that are beyond your control. Many of the strategies described in this book are coping strategies that can be useful when things go wrong. Some of these strategies include:

➤ Challenging shoulds, thinking errors and other unhelpful self-talk that contribute to upsetting emotions when problems arise.
➤ Talking to people who are supportive.
➤ Using relaxation and mindfulness techniques to help us feel calmer.
➤ Getting involved in enjoyable activities, so we don't keep continuously focusing on our problem.

PRACTISE ACCEPTANCE

There are many things that we don't like that are beyond our control. For example, there isn't much we can do about our height, our age, most of our physical features or the family we were born into. There are also things that have happened in the past that we can't erase: an essay or exam that we failed, an argument that we had with someone, our parents getting divorced or a close friend moving away. What has happened has happened, and we can't change it.

The best way to deal with situations we can't change is to practise acceptance. This means 'going with' the way things are, without internally insisting that they should be different. At the same time, we make a commitment to ourselves to get on with other aspects, so that we can still have meaningful lives, in spite of things not being exactly as we would like. The following acceptance affirmation summarises it well:

Acceptance

This is how it is.

Not how it:

− was

− might have been

− should have been

Not how I:

− want it to be

− planned it to be

− hoped it would be

I accept that this is how it is.

And now I get on with my life in a positive way.

VESNA'S boyfriend broke off their relationship after they had been together for six months. Vesna felt devastated and tried several strategies to get him back, but they did not work. Finally, she realised that there was nothing more she could do — he was not going to change his mind. For the next two months, Vesna went through a period of grief. Sometimes, she felt sad; at other times, angry, frustrated and depressed. However, gradually, Vesna started to accept the situation. While she continued to feel sad at times, most of her overthinking and overanalysing stopped. The process of acceptance enabled her to start thinking about other parts of her life. As a result, Vesna began going out more with her friends, getting back to the hockey and the social justice groups she used to enjoy, and focusing on her school work again. Recognising that all the analysing she was doing was pointless, and would not change the situation, helped Vesna to reach the point of acceptance.

NATHAN has bad asthma. He hates it, because he always has to take medication and he finds the asthma attacks stressful. Nathan spends a lot of time thinking about how much better his life would be if he didn't have asthma. The problem is that, while he can take daily tablets and use a puffer to help keep it under control, there is nothing he can do to get rid of it all together. Like many people who have difficulty with acceptance, Nathan believes that if he stops thinking about his asthma, it will never go away. At some deeper level, it feels like as long as he is worrying about it, he is doing something about the problem. Of course, Nathan will tell you that, rationally, he knows this belief is crazy, but on a 'gut level' it feels true. Part of the process of working towards acceptance is reminding himself that overthinking and overanalysing does not help his asthma. It is possible that he may grow out of it as he gets older, or that a medical cure may be found further down the track but, for now, there is nothing he can do. Nathan decides to relax into the reality of his situation. 'It is what it is, and now I get on with my life in a positive way.'

Reflect

Is there a situation that you don't like, but which you cannot change?

How much time do you spend thinking about it? Is your thinking helpful?

If you were able to fully accept this situation, and no longer think about it, what difference would this make to the way you feel?

IN A NUTSHELL ...

➤ Problems are a normal part of life. Taking action to resolve problems can help us to get our needs met more often and gives us a sense of control.

➤ When no obvious solutions to our problems exist, it may be helpful to go through a step-by-step problem-solving process.

➤ In situations where we cannot solve particular problems, our best option is usually to practise acceptance. This frees our mind to focus on other parts of our lives.

Step-by-step problem-solving guide

Step 1: Define the problem (be specific).

Step 2: Work out your goals for this problem (be realistic).

Step 3: Brainstorm possible solutions to the problem (don't judge them yet).

Step 4: Rule out impractical or unrealistic options.

Step 5: Identify the 'pros' and 'cons' of your remaining options

    a. Pros:

       Cons:

    b. Pros:

       Cons:

    c. Pros:

       Cons:

    d. Pros:

       Cons:

    e. Pros:

       Cons:

Step 6: Identify your best options.

Step 7: Implement the best options.

Step 8: Evaluate the results.

TWELVE

Effective Communication

The way we communicate has a major impact on our ability to get on with people and get our needs met. Good communication skills can help us to solve problems and avoid conflict. They enable us to express our thoughts, feelings and concerns in a way that increases our chances of getting a positive response from others. Open and honest communication is important for developing quality friendships and having healthy relationships with others.

STYLES OF COMMUNICATION

When we look at different types of communication, they usually fit into one of three styles: aggressive, passive or assertive.

AGGRESSIVE COMMUNICATION

Aggressive communication is expressed in an unfriendly or hostile manner, and usually involves alienating messages such as 'you-statements' (blaming the other person, or implying they are wrong or at fault) and labelling. The tone of voice and facial expressions may also convey hostility. The assumption behind aggressive communication is 'Your needs don't matter' (*I win/you lose*).

PASSIVE COMMUNICATION

Passive communication involves putting our own needs last. We don't express our thoughts or feelings, or ask for what we want. When we use passive communication, it feels like others are walking all over us, because we don't assert our own needs. If we bottle things up for too long, we may end up feeling resentful. The assumption behind passive communication is 'My needs don't matter' (*you win/I lose*).

ASSERTIVE COMMUNICATION

Assertive communication involves clearly expressing what we think, feel and/or want, without being pushy or demanding that things must go our way. The underlying assumption is 'We both matter — let's try to work this out' (*I win/you win*). Assertive communication increases our chances of getting our needs met, avoiding clashes with others and maintaining positive relationships.

When we are assertive, we can:

➤ express our thoughts, feelings and needs
➤ make reasonable requests of other people (while accepting their right to say 'no')
➤ stand up for our rights when appropriate
➤ say 'no' to requests from others at times, without feeling guilty.

COMMUNICATION PROBLEMS

Poor communication is a major source of tension and negativity within relationships. It creates misunderstanding and conflict in all sorts of situations, and may leave us feeling stressed and disconnected.

Communication problems arise for many reasons. These include inadequate communication skills, feeling overly defensive and therefore not listening to what the other person is saying, feeling angry and therefore communicating aggressively, or missing parts of the other person's message because we are preoccupied with our own thoughts.

TONY is feeling angry. He is due to go for his provisional driver's licence next week and for the past month his dad has been promising to take him driving, but has never got around to it. Tony is worried that if he doesn't get more practice before he goes for the test, he will fail. On Thursday, Tony came home from school and asked his dad if they could go for a drive. His dad said he couldn't because he had to finish up some work. Well, Tony just saw red and exploded: 'You don't give a damn about me. You are such a liar! You never do what you say you are going to do.' In response, his dad got completely fired up, called him a 'spoilt brat' and said that Tony never thought about anyone but himself.

This is a good example of how poor communication can lead to conflict and bad feelings. Let's take a look at some of the errors that led to the angry outburst.

MISTAKE NUMBER 1: MAKING ASSUMPTIONS

Up until their argument, his dad had no idea how important it was to Tony to get the extra driving practice. He thought that Tony felt confident about the test and assumed he just wanted to go for a drive for fun, which was something they could do anytime. Tony, on the other hand, had assumed that his father knew how important it was for him to get some more practice (even though he never told him). As a result, he interpreted his dad's attitude as not caring.

Often we expect people to know what we think, even though we have not told them directly. For example, we might expect someone to realise that what they are doing annoys us, even though we haven't actually said as much. So a vital component of good communication is to *tell others what you think and want; don't assume that they already know!*

In Tony's case, the situation may have turned out better if he had told his dad what he was thinking and feeling: 'Dad, I've got my driver's licence test on Tuesday and I'm feeling nervous about it. I'm worried I haven't had enough experience on the road and might fail the test. Can we organise to go for a few drives this week? Do you have some time to take me? When would suit you best?'

By clearly communicating how important getting some driving practice is to him, Tony would give his dad a better understanding of where he is coming from. Scheduling a specific time strengthens the commitment and makes it easier for both of them to plan ahead.

MISTAKE NUMBER 2: AVOIDING COMMUNICATION

Tony left it until he was seething with anger before he said anything to his dad. In the weeks before, each time his dad cancelled the planned driving practice, Tony said nothing. Over time, he stewed about it more and more, and finally he exploded. This type of situation is a bit like boiling water in a pot with the lid on — if you don't let off a bit of steam as you go along, eventually the pressure builds up and it boils over. *Whenever we're feeling upset, it is better to talk about it*, rather than saying nothing and letting things escalate.

Communication problems often arise because we don't say how we feel, what we think or what we want. People often avoid communicating because they are uncomfortable, or worried about a negative reaction. Sometimes we just assume that others should know what we think. The problem is that when we don't say what we need to say, we feel angry, resentful and frustrated. This can lead to tension in our relationships and, sometimes, to angry explosions.

MISTAKE NUMBER 3: LABELLING

Another problem with the communication between Tony and his dad is that they both used *labels* to criticise each other (e.g. *'You are a liar'*, *'You are a spoilt brat'*). When we label another person, they feel under attack, and usually their first reaction is to attack back (just like Tony's dad did). This leads to heated arguments and conflict. Labels are unhelpful because they condemn the person, rather than their behaviour. It is OK to criticise someone's behaviour (e.g. 'I think what you did was unfair') but when we label the person (e.g. 'You are pathetic'), it feels like a personal attack. This puts the other person on the defensive, and often creates hostility and other bad feelings.

MISTAKE NUMBER 4: ALIENATING MESSAGES

When we use criticism, put-downs or aggressive communication, nobody wins — everyone feels bad in the end. Alienating messages make the other person feel threatened or under attack. These messages often lead to heated confrontations or a 'cold war' (where you stop speaking to each other, or use minimal communication).

Some examples of alienating messages include:

➤ **You-statements:** We blame the other person and accuse them of being wrong or at fault. For example, Tony telling his dad, 'You don't give a damn about me!'

➤ **Sarcasm:** We deliberately mock someone, by saying one thing, but meaning the opposite. For example, 'Well, we can't all be perfect like you!' or 'You're spending all that time on the internet — you are obviously going to get As for all your exams so you don't need to study.'

➤ **Negative comparisons:** We compare the person to someone else to make them look bad. For example, 'Sharon's mum makes an effort — she always looks so young [unlike you!]' or 'Your sister always gets As on her report [so why can't you?]'

➤ **Threats:** We threaten there will be some kind of punishment if we don't get our way. For example, 'If you don't do what I want, I'm going to leave home/never talk to you again/be rude to your boyfriend.'

The communication problems between Tony and his father are very common. Can you think of some examples where you or someone you know has engaged in communication errors (such as making assumptions, avoidance or alienating messages)? It is often useful to reflect on our communication style, so that we can avoid getting caught up in these unhelpful patterns.

STRATEGIES FOR EFFECTIVE COMMUNICATION

Communication can be enhanced by using clear, non-confrontational statements like 'whole messages' or 'I-statements'. In addition, using appropriate timing, effective body language and tone of voice can also improve our communication. These strategies are explained below.

USE WHOLE MESSAGES

In their book *Messages: The Communications Skills Book*, authors McKay, Davis and Fanning describe a method of communication using *whole messages*. This method is particularly useful when we want to communicate about an issue that could create tension or conflict. A whole message involves expressing how you think and feel, and what you would like. It consists of four parts: observations, thoughts, feelings and wants.

OBSERVATIONS

This is a factual account of what happened (not your own interpretation). To keep it objective, it can be helpful to ask yourself, 'What would someone else have observed if they had been a fly on the wall?'

For example:

1. 'The other day when Mike came over, you didn't stop and talk to him.'
2. 'Last weekend, I lent you my white dress to wear to Mia's party and you gave it back to me unwashed, and with a stain on it.'

THOUGHTS

This is your own opinion or interpretation of what happened. You are communicating your point of view.

For example:

1. 'I thought it was a bit rude — it looked as though you don't like him.'
2. 'It seemed to me like you didn't care about my dress, and that you weren't prepared to make an effort to return it in the state that you received it.'

FEELINGS

You let the other person how you feel about the situation — your emotional reaction.

For example:

1. 'I felt embarrassed and uncomfortable.'
2. 'I felt disappointed and annoyed.'

WANTS

You tell the other person what you would like to happen in the situation. You are not demanding that they do something (which is unlikely to get a positive response). Instead, you are making a request.

For example:

1. 'Next time Mike comes over, I'd like you say "Hi" and make an effort to chat with him.'
2. 'I would like you to clean the dress — either handwash it or get it dry-cleaned.'

Let's take a look at how Tony could have communicated with his dad using a whole message:

➤ *Tony's observations:* 'In the past month, you have agreed to take me out driving on at least three occasions, but each time something came up and we didn't go.'

➤ *Tony's thoughts/feelings:* 'I feel upset that you've cancelled so many times. I know you are busy, but this is important to me. I'm going for my licence next week, and I'm worried that I'll fail if I don't get some more practice.'

➤ *Tony's wants:* 'I would really like us to make a time to go for a drive, and for you to stick to the arrangement.'

Exercise

Learning to communicate effectively takes a bit of practice. Here are some examples of situations you can use to hone your communication skills. Have a go at writing whole messages, as demonstrated above.

Remember to describe:

a. Your observations — what actually happened.

b. Your thoughts and/or feelings — what you think and/or how you feel.

c. Your wants — what would you like to happen.

(Sample solutions at the end of the chapter.)

Situation 1: Your friend introduced you to a boy named Jimmy but, as you were involved in a conversation with another person at the time, you didn't make a big effort to talk to him. Now you're feeling anxious that you may have behaved poorly and you would like your friend to know that you didn't mean to be rude.

Observations:

Thoughts/feelings:

Wants:

Situation 2: A friend borrowed your favourite jacket from you more than a month ago and she has not mentioned it again, or offered to give it back. You would like it returned.

Observations:

Thoughts/feelings:

Wants:

Situation 3: One of your friends has the habit of calling very late at night. Your parents are not impressed and have already asked you a few times to tell him not to call so late. You want to communicate this to him.

Observations:

Thoughts/feelings:

Wants:

Now try it for yourself. Think of a situation that you have experienced in the past (or currently), where you needed to communicate with someone about an issue of concern. Describe the situation and who you need to communicate with.

Now, write the whole message.
Observations:

Thoughts/feelings:

Wants:

If you are finding it difficult to raise an issue directly with a person, it can be helpful to take some time to think through and write down the whole message first. This gives you an opportunity to plan what you want to say and how to say it.

USE 'I-STATEMENTS'

As we saw earlier, 'you-statements' put people on the defensive and typically escalate tension. 'I-statements', on the other hand, usually have the opposite effect. When we point the finger at ourselves (rather than the other person), we take ownership of our feelings and concerns, and *avoid blaming them*. If we use this approach, people are more likely to be receptive to what we have to say.

For example:

➤ 'I feel disappointed that you cancelled at the last minute', rather than 'You've let me down again'.

➤ 'I feel frustrated when you don't pass on my messages', rather than 'You never pass on my messages'.

➤ 'I felt upset about what you said earlier', rather than 'You make me so angry'.

DON'T DROP HINTS — BE CLEAR

When we hint at something rather than make a clear statement, people don't always get the message. Similarly, when we ramble on instead of being direct, it is easy for the main message to get lost. So if there is something you need to say, state it clearly — don't hint at it.

> *TRAN is hoping to spend some time with Lauren, who he has recently started seeing. He calls her and causally asks what she has on over the weekend. Lauren says she has an assignment to finish and a family dinner. Tran ends the conversation feeling disappointed. He concludes that Lauren is not really into him. Instead of clearly communicating what he wanted ('I would like to catch up with you this weekend. Are you free?'), Tran hinted by asking Lauren what she was up to and assumed that she would read between the lines. Lauren had assumed Tran must be busy or not too keen to see her, otherwise he would have asked her to meet up.*

DO IT NOW

If there is an issue you need to raise, or a situation that needs to be resolved, try to deal with it as soon as possible. The longer you leave it, the harder it gets, and the less likely it is to be fixed. The only exception to this rule is when you feel very angry, in which case it is wise to give yourself a 'cooling-off' period first. This reduces the likelihood of conflict, or saying something you might regret later.

ASK FOR CLARIFICATION

Just as people can't always read our minds, sometimes it is difficult for us to interpret what they are thinking or feeling. If you are confused about the message you are receiving, check it out with the other person. For example, if a friend seems quiet and withdrawn when you see them, instead of suspecting they might be angry with you, ask them: 'You seem quiet today — have I done something to upset you?' or 'Is everything OK?' These types of questions can bring unresolved issues to the surface and open up the chance to talk things through. If, however, there is nothing wrong, talking about it can be reassuring and ease your concerns.

ACKNOWLEDGE YOUR DISCOMFORT

If you feel uncomfortable raising a particular issue, it may be helpful to let the other person know this. For example: 'Look, George, I feel really uneasy bringing this up, but ...' or 'Katie, I need to talk to you about something and I'm feeling nervous about it. I don't want to hurt your feelings, but if I don't say anything, I know I'm just going to continue feeling upset.' By honestly disclosing your discomfort, you 'lower the temperature' and reduce the likelihood that the other person will become hostile or defensive.

BE AWARE OF YOUR BODY LANGUAGE

The way you speak — including the volume and tone of your voice, your physical gestures and your facial expressions — has an important impact on how your message will be received. For example, if you fold your arms in front of your chest, frown and speak in an accusing tone, the other person is likely to feel defensive, even before they have heard what you have to say. On the other hand, an open posture, a calm voice and relaxed body language encourages the other person to feel at ease, and your message can be delivered in a non-threatening way.

COMMUNICATE POSITIVE FEELINGS

Developing good relationships means being able to express positive feelings at times. We often assume that people are aware that we like them, or that they know we appreciate what they do for us, so we don't mention it. However, people aren't mind-readers, and if we don't tell them they don't always know. Even if they do know, everyone likes to hear someone say nice things about them every now and then! Communicating positive feelings towards others lets them know that we value them, and helps to strengthen bonds.

Warm feelings can also be expressed as a whole message. For example: 'Maria, the other day when I was upset, you sat down and asked me if I was OK. It was really good to talk to you — I appreciate your concern. I just wanted to say thanks — you've been a supportive friend.'

Alternatively, we can communicate warm feelings by making simple statements such as: 'Thanks for being there for me the other day' or 'You've been a caring friend — I really appreciate it.'

Reflect

Is there someone you would like to give some positive feedback to? What could you say to them?

IN A NUTSHELL ...

➤ Good communication skills can help us have healthy relationships, avoid conflict and solve problems.

➤ Tensions can arise in relationships when we make assumptions, give unclear messages, avoid saying what we need to say, or communicate in an alienating or hostile manner.

➤ Effective communication strategies, such as whole messages and 'I-statements', can help us resolve problems and disagreements in a reasonable and respectful way.

Sample solutions to 'whole messages' exercise on page 164–65

Situation 1: Your friend introduced you to a boy named Jimmy, but as you were involved in a conversation with another person at the time, you didn't make a big effort to talk to him. Now you're feeling anxious that you may have behaved poorly and you would like your friend to know that you didn't mean to be rude.

Observations: Last night when you introduced me to Jimmy, I hardly spoke to him.

Thoughts/feelings: I'm feeling bad, because I was caught up in a conversation I was having and I think I may have come across as rude.

Wants: Could you let Jimmy know that I'm sorry if I seemed rude? I will certainly be more welcoming next time.

Situation 2: A friend borrowed something from you more than a month ago, and she has not mentioned it or offered to give it back. You would like it returned.

Observations: Last month you borrowed my jacket and you haven't given it back yet.

Thoughts/feelings: It is my favourite jacket and I'm really missing it.

Wants: Would you be able to bring it to school tomorrow, so that I can have it back in time for the weekend?

Situation 3: One of your friends has the habit of calling very late at night. Your parents are not impressed and have already asked you a few times to tell him not to call so late. You want to communicate this to him.

Observations: Over the past few weeks, you have called me after 10.30 pm quite a few times.

Thoughts/feelings: I'm finding it hard, because Mum and Dad are having a go at me about it. It also doesn't work for me because I've got swimming training early in the mornings.

Wants: You're welcome to call, but can you make sure that it is before 9 pm?

CHAPTER 13

Setting Goals

Have you ever wondered what is really important to you? What do you value and want to achieve? For instance, it might be having close and supportive friendships, being the best you can be at your favourite sport, finding a career you enjoy, having a healthy lifestyle, making a difference on some issue that matters to you, or taking on a new challenge.

When our personal values guide our choices and goals, we tend to feel energised and positive about where we are heading. Setting goals helps us transform our values into achievements. They give us direction and help us attain the things we want, in both the near and distant future. Goals motivate us to channel our time and energy into things that matter to us. Making progress towards our goals gives us a sense of accomplishment and can create feelings of excitement and confidence.

Take some time to think about the things you would like to achieve over the next year or two. If nothing springs to mind, try closing your eyes and imagining what you would like your life to look like in one or two years' time. What would you like to be doing? How would you like to be feeling? What do you hope will be different?

Here are some areas in which you might consider setting goals:

➤ Personal qualities (e.g. becoming more confident, assertive or relaxed)

➤ Friendships/relationships

➤ Family

➤ Work/study/career
➤ Physical health
➤ Interests/hobbies
➤ Attitudes

Let's take a look at the goals identified by Liam and Casey when they did this exercise:

LIAM'S goals
Where I would like to be in one year:
➤ *Personal qualities: I would like to be completely over my depression.*
➤ *Interests/hobbies: I would like to be a competent surfer.*
➤ *Work/study/career: I would like to be doing work experience in web design.*

CASEY'S goals
Where I would like to be in two years' time:
➤ *Work/study/career: I would like to be studying arts at uni.*
➤ *Friendships/relationships: I would like to have at least three close friends that I can rely on.*
➤ *Physical health: I would like to be doing some type of exercise at least five times a week.*
➤ *Personal qualities: I would like to be able to stay relatively calm, even when under pressure.*

Reflect
Take a look at the list of areas in which you might consider setting goals on previous page. Choose one or two areas that are important to you and write something you would like to achieve under these headings. For the rest of this chapter, we'll look at strategies you can use to work towards achieving these goals.

STRATEGIES TO ACHIEVE GOALS

A helpful approach to achieving goals involves three basic steps:

Step 1: Define your goal

Step 2: Set subgoals

Step 3: Create and work through a plan of action

STEP 1: DEFINE YOUR GOAL

Think about what you would like to achieve and write it down. When you do this, keep in mind the following things:

MAKE SURE YOUR GOAL IS SPECIFIC

Define your goal in specific rather than vague terms. For instance, 'to be happier' is a vague goal and is difficult to measure. How will you know when you are there? To make your goal specific, think about specific outcomes; for example, 'I would like to wake up every morning without a knot in my stomach', 'I would like to attend school every day, except when I am genuinely sick', or 'I would like to catch up with friends on the weekends'. With more specific goals, you can more clearly see whether or not you have achieved them.

SET A TIME FRAME

Giving yourself a deadline is important, because it keeps you focused and motivated. Without a deadline, you might find yourself putting it off, getting caught up in other things and eventually losing sight of your goal.

MAKE SURE YOUR GOAL IS REALISTIC

Most people have the capacity to achieve a lot more than they actually do, and sometimes it's good to push yourself beyond your comfort zone. On the other hand, it's also important not to set goals that are unachievable.

Having unrealistically high expectations increases your likelihood of failure, which can in turn dampen your enthusiasm. It can also put unnecessary pressure on yourself. For example, if you are a Year 12 student, aiming to be the dux of the state (or even dux of the school) might be unrealistic. However, working towards getting scores above eighty per cent in your final results may be a reasonable goal, if it is within your academic capability. While this goal will keep you motivated, it is far less likely to cause panic and burnout than striving to be top of the school or state.

MAKE SURE YOUR GOAL IS MEANINGFUL

You are more likely to succeed when your goal is relevant and meaningful to you. Don't fall into the trap of taking on other people's goals.

VLAD'S dad loves cars and wants Vlad to follow him in becoming a mechanic. Although Vlad has little interest in cars, and would prefer a career in the performing arts, he sets himself a goal to find a mechanics apprenticeship, in order to please his dad. As this is not something he genuinely wants for himself, Vlad is not excited or motivated to pursue it.

STEP 2: SET SUBGOALS

Subgoals are the specific steps we take to achieve our main goal. When you define subgoals, it gives you a path to follow. Once you start working through your subgoals, you get the sense that you are making progress. Ticking the boxes as you achieve each subgoal also gives you a psychological boost.

Below are examples of main goals selected by Liam and Casey, and the subgoals that they set for each goal.

CASEY'S GOAL	SUBGOALS
To have at least three close friends that I can rely on by the end of the year	Make more effort to stay in touch with my existing friends, e.g. call Marisa or Luc at least once a week. Return people's calls when they phone me. Invite friends to hang out, watch a movie or have a BBQ. Go to at least one event per week where I might meet new people (e.g. join a club, play sport, etc.). Try to be more open and honest when I'm talking to people that I like.

LIAM'S GOAL	SUBGOALS
To be over my depression in two months' time.	Do three things each day that give me some pleasure.
	Do three things each day that give me a feeling of achievement.
	Talk to Mum, Dad and my friend Mark about how I am feeling.
	Walk the dog every day after school, even when I don't feel like it.
	Use my mood journal app to monitor my mood, and reflect on what I am thinking.
	Fill out a Stress Log and dispute faulty thinking and negative thoughts when I'm feeling down about something.
	Practice 20 minutes of mindfulness meditation every day.
	Write down my achievements at the end of each day, even when they seem really minor.

STEP 3: CREATE AND WORK THROUGH A PLAN OF ACTION

The third stage is to write a step-by-step plan of action for achieving each subgoal and, ultimately, your main goal. This includes setting deadlines for each subgoal and writing down all the 'nitty-gritty' things you are going to do today, tomorrow and later this week to achieve each subgoal. Think of your goals and subgoals as being your target destinations, and your plan of action as being the finer detail map that shows you how to get there.

The following is Liam's plan of action for his goal to become a competent surfer:

MY GOAL:

To be a competent surfer by the end of the year.
This specifically means I will be able to paddle out, duck dive and get to my feet on most waves I catch.

HOW WILL I BENEFIT FROM ACHIEVING THIS GOAL?
➤ I will enjoy it.
➤ It will help me to stay fit.

➤ It's sociable — something I can do with my friends.

➤ It's a skill and getting better at it will give me a sense of achievement.

SPECIFIC STEPS TO ACHIEVE THIS GOAL:

SUBGOALS	TARGET DATE
Ask Mum and Dad to pay for three surfing lessons as part of my birthday present.	Tonight
Join the local board riders club and go in their monthly competitions.	By Tuesday 2 May
Go out with my brother Dom, who is good at it, and get him to give me some tips at least once a week.	Regularly, starting 4 May
Go surfing a minimum of three times a week (at least two mornings before school and once on the weekend).	Starting 4 May

THE NITTY-GRITTY (THINGS I NEED TO DO THIS WEEK):

❏ Tonight: Talk to Mum and Dad about surfing lessons.

❏ Talk to Dom about going surfing with him.

❏ Tomorrow: Contact the local board riders club and find out about membership.

❏ Wednesday: Book my surfing lessons for Monday and Friday of next week.

❏ Tell Steve and Bruce that I want to join them when they go surfing on Monday and Friday mornings, once I've had my lessons.

For longer-term goals, it is helpful to consider other timeframes. For example, what needs to happen in the next month, three months or six months to keep you going? When you are aiming for something in the more distant future, completing a 'nitty gritty' plan-of-action sheet each week until your deadline is reached may increase your chances of achieving your final goal.

Reflect

Choose one of the goals that you identified earlier. In the form below, describe it as a specific goal and set a deadline for its achievement. Then fill in the rest of the form, describing the benefits you stand to gain, your subgoals and the steps you need to take this week in working towards your goal.

Plan of Action

My goal

How will I benefit from achieving this goal?

Specific steps to achieve this goal

SUBGOALS	TARGET DATE

The nitty-gritty (things I need to do this week)

IDENTIFY OBSTACLES

Once we have defined our goals, worked out subgoals and come up with a plan of action, we are well on our way to achieving what we want. But it's not always smooth sailing from here. Sometimes, despite our best intentions, obstacles get in the way. Obstacles can be practical problems, such as:

➤ Not having enough time
➤ Not having enough money
➤ Lacking the necessary knowledge or skills
➤ Being stressed and fatigued
➤ Having parents or friends who don't approve of your goal

Obstacles can also be psychological blocks, such as:

➤ Fear of failure
➤ Fear of disapproval or rejection
➤ Lack of confidence in your ability to succeed
➤ Frustration
➤ Lack of motivation
➤ Short attention span (or difficulty staying focused)
➤ Lack of a well-defined goal

Obstacles don't necessarily stop us from achieving our goals, but they present a roadblock. They challenge us to work out strategies to overcome them. It is helpful to think ahead, to identify any difficulties that might arise and consider how we can address them.

Let's take a look at Casey's plan for dealing with possible obstacles in relation to doing regular exercise.

CASEY'S GOAL: TO EXERCISE AT LEAST FIVE TIMES A WEEK

POSSIBLE OBSTACLES	STRATEGIES TO OVERCOME THEM
I find it hard to get out of bed early in the morning.	Set my alarm for 6 am. Put positive statements on the bedside table for me to see when I open my eyes, e.g. 'I can do this' and 'No pain, no gain!' Have my sports gear laid out on my dressing table. Get straight into it when the alarm goes. Don't think about it, just do it. Make sure I am out the door by 6.20 am.
I'll get bored and then lose my motivation.	Vary my exercise (e.g. try different running routes, occasionally run on the bush track, do an aerobics class at the gym each week, cycle once a week). Talk to Mum and my sister Annie about training together on some mornings. Make a playlist of my favourite energising tracks and listen to it while I'm exercising.
I might lose sight of my goal over time.	Keep that photo of me jogging on the beach next to my clock, so that I am reminded of how good it feels to be fit. Train with Mum and/or Annie, so that I have a commitment to someone else (not just me). Sign up to do the ten-kilometre fun run with Annie in September.

Reflect

In the table below, list all the possible obstacles that might get in the way of achieving your goal and strategies that you can use to overcome them.

My goal:

POSSIBLE OBSTACLES	STRATEGIES TO OVERCOME THEM

STAYING MOTIVATED

You have defined your goal, set subgoals and have been working on them for a while. But now, with lots of school assignments due, exams coming up and life just getting busy, it's easy to get distracted. Many people lose sight of their goals because other things get in the way. For this reason, it is helpful to think about strategies that will help to keep you focused and motivated over time. Below are some things you can do to maintain motivation.

FOCUS ON THE REWARDS

Thinking about the rewards you stand to gain can help to maintain motivation, especially if it makes you feel excited. For this reason, it may be helpful to write down the benefits of achieving your goal. Think creatively when you write your list. Besides the direct benefits of achieving what you want, there may also be the satisfaction of feeling in control, a stronger belief in your ability to get things done, and perhaps even greater self-confidence.

Reflect

Choose one of the goals you identified earlier and write down all the benefits that you stand to gain by achieving that goal:

VISUALISE SUCCESS

Research suggests that we are more likely to perform a new behaviour if we have visualised it repeatedly in our mind. Visualising can make us feel excited about our goal and frequent visualisation helps to keep it at the front of our mind. It is helpful to visualise the final outcome you are seeking, as well as the steps you will need to take along the way. You can visualise your goals while doing physical exercise, when going to sleep at night or whenever you have some downtime.

USE REMINDERS

The more often you think about your goal, the more it stays in your mind. Displaying photos, images from the web or inspirational statements that represent what you want to achieve can keep you inspired and focused.

> *Casey put a photo of herself and a friend at the finishing line of the school cross-country race as her phone screensaver. In the photo, both she and her friend have smiles on their faces, and Casey remembers how happy she felt that she had managed to complete the distance. The photo comes up several times a day and, each time, she takes a few moments to pause and look at it. She also put a sign saying 'Feeling fit and fabulous' on the wall above her desk.*

TALK ABOUT IT

The very act of talking about goals and how you plan to achieve them can be inspiring and strengthen motivation. This is particularly the case if others support and encourage you in the process. Verbally expressing your goals adds an extra level of processing, and reinforces your intention and planning. Sometimes people might give you ideas or inspiration, while at other times it is just the process of describing your goal that is most beneficial. There is also a feeling of commitment that comes with telling others what you intend to do. This may be reinforced when, down the track, they ask you about how things are progressing.

IN A NUTSHELL ...

➤ Setting goals keeps us focused and motivated, and increases our chances of getting the things we want.

➤ In order to achieve our goals, it is helpful to clearly define what we want, set subgoals to work towards along the way, and follow a step-by-step plan of action.

➤ When planning goals, it is important to consider the potential obstacles and work out a plan to overcome them. To stay motivated, consider focusing on the potential rewards of achieving your goal, visualising success, using graphic or written reminders and sharing your vision with others.

FOURTEEN

Self-care

Have you ever stayed up super late doing last-minute cramming for an exam, then found yourself really struggling the following day? Has taking yourself off for a run when you're feeling stressed ever left you feeling a whole lot better? Has spending hours online without a break ever resulted in 'brain fog'? Or has calling a friend when you're going through a rough patch ever lifted your mood?

Our minds and bodies are connected. Our thoughts and emotions have a direct effect on our bodies and, conversely, the things that happen in our bodies have a direct effect on our mental states.

Self-care is about taking action to look after yourself, both physically and mentally. Positive self-care choices can make a real difference to your mood and emotions, and therefore to your ability to deal with life's challenges. For teenagers, there are some key areas of self-care that are particularly important.

SLEEP

Cast your mind back over the last week. What time did you go to bed and what time did you wake up each day? How much sleep did you get each night?

Experts claim that for 'optimal' functioning (that is, to feel energised and perform well), teenagers need between nine and ten hours of sleep per night. It's probably no surprise that most teens get much less than that. In fact, research shows that adolescents are one of the most sleep-deprived groups in the world.

Sleep is essential for healthy brain functioning. It provides an opportunity for our brains to click the 'refresh' button after the day's activity. During sleep, we process what we have learned and lay down memories.

Sleep deprivation alters the activity of the brain, making it hard to concentrate, especially in situations that require sustained focus (not so helpful when you are working on a complex assignment or wanting to give a friend your undivided attention during a deep and meaningful conversation). Sleep deprivation reduces energy and motivation, and makes it difficult to problem-solve and make decisions. In contrast, you have probably noticed how much more alert and on top of things you feel after a good night's sleep.

If sleep debt (not getting enough sleep) is an issue for you, it could be for a number of reasons. As a teenager, you might have a hectic schedule. With school, homework, part-time jobs, family time, after-school activities and a social life … who has time for sleep, right? We tend to prioritise almost everything else over getting to bed at a decent hour. Aside from all these commitments, it's also easy to get caught up watching TV, scrolling through social media or just checking out the latest online videos. Sometimes you are just so into what you are doing that you don't want to stop, even though the clock keeps ticking. There may also be lots of thoughts going around inside your head and, even though your body feels tired, it is hard to switch off your mind.

Many teenagers also notice changes in their body clock. Chances are you find it harder to wake up in the mornings than you did when you were younger, and you don't start feeling tired until much later in the evening. Your biology may be partly responsible for this. During adolescence, your brain starts to release melatonin (the hormone responsible for bringing on sleepiness) later and later. This is not much help if you don't feel like going to bed but still need to be up and ready early in the morning for school or other commitments.

If these issues are relevant for you, here are some things that you can do to address them:

➤ *Make sleep a priority*: Remind yourself how much better you feel after enough shut-eye, and use this as motivation to turn off the TV or finish whatever you are doing and head to bed. Going to bed at the same time each night, and having a consistent wake-up time in the morning, will help you get into a routine. If you are in the habit of going to bed late, you can retrain yourself by gradually going to bed a little earlier each night (say five or ten minutes). This will allow your body to adjust to a healthier sleep schedule.

➤ *Make sure your room is dark and quiet* when you go to bed. This sends a message to your brain that it is sleep time.

➤ *Avoid using electronic devices* at least half an hour before you go to bed. Artificial light from screens send signals to the brain that 'It's light, so it must be daytime — stay awake!' This delays the production of melatonin (the sleepiness hormone), making it harder to fall asleep.

➤ *Minimise possible distractions.* Have you ever been drifting off to sleep when your phone suddenly beeps or a message pops up on your computer screen? These can jolt you out of sleep mode and get your brain and body revved up again. Turn off your devices before bed, or switch them to silent. Putting them out of reach can also help you resist the temptation to check in with what's happening online when you are meant to be sleeping.

➤ *Give yourself some chill-out time.* For half an hour to an hour before bed, have some quiet time. Having a shower or bath, reading a book in bed or putting on some relaxing music can help set the stage for sleep. This lets your body and brain know that it is time to start winding down. During this time, try to avoid anything that gets the adrenaline pumping or your brain fired up (including video games or high-drama TV shows).

➤ *Keep a pen and pad beside your bed* and write down any repetitive worries that keep you awake at night. Remind yourself that you will follow up on these issues in the morning, but not now. The middle of the night is never a good time to solve problems; it's hard to be objective, because your brain produces more catastrophic thoughts at this time. When you revisit the issue on the following day, you might find that it's not so important and wasn't worth wasting your sleep time on.

PHYSICAL EXERCISE

People who exercise regularly have lower levels of depression and anxiety than those who don't. Getting yourself moving creates changes in brain chemistry that positively affect how you feel. Intense exercise (like jogging, swimming or cycling) triggers the release of *endorphins* in the brain. These 'feel-good' chemicals enhance your mood and may be the reason some people describe experiencing a 'runner's high' after a hard workout. Exercise also increases levels of *serotonin*, another brain chemical associated with positive mood and better sleep. It also reduces levels of stress hormones, including adrenaline and cortisol.

A further benefit of exercise is that it distracts you from rumination and unhelpful thoughts. When you are in the middle of a game of soccer or netball, your mind is focused on things happening right now, so it becomes disconnected from overthinking and rumination. Getting active with other people also has a social dimension, which makes it more enjoyable. If the exercise you do incorporates a 'fun factor', such as chatting to a friend while you walk, or practising your signature move at the skate ramp, this too can lift your spirits. An exercise buzz can be magnified by a sense of achievement, like when you make it through a tough class at the gym, or reach your goal of swimming twenty laps of the pool.

With exercise, it helps to have a plan. If you have a clear idea of what activity you are going to do and when you are going to do it, it's much more likely to happen. However, any amount of exercise is better than none. You don't need to become a marathon runner or a gym junkie to benefit. Just getting yourself moving more during the day will make a difference. Take the stairs instead of the escalator when you have the option. Walk to the shops instead of waiting for a lift. Get off the bus one or two stops early and walk the extra distance. Aim to do at least thirty minutes of moderate exercise on most days.

Exercise doesn't have to be a chore and it doesn't have to be too serious. It can be as simple as putting on music and dancing around in your lounge room, or diving into the ocean and body surfing some waves. Choosing activities that you enjoy will keep you motivated and combining it with socialising can make it more fun. Why not get a few people together for a weekend kick-around at a nearby park, or join a sports team so you can meet new people and get fit at the same time?

HEALTHY EATING

A healthy and balanced diet will benefit your physical health, as well as your emotional well-being. Choosing nutrient-rich foods that are not highly processed, and eating at regular intervals throughout the day, will help maintain energy levels and make a real difference to how you feel.

Our blood-sugar levels can have a significant influence on our mood. Food and drinks that are refined and high in sugar (such as cakes, lollies and soft drinks) are quickly absorbed into the bloodstream, resulting in a rapid-onset energy rush. This can provide a temporary pep-up. The downside, however, is that the surge does not last and is followed by a dip in blood-sugar levels, which creates an energy slump. These highs and lows can send us on a roller-coaster ride of emotions: from a big boost to feeling wiped out and irritable as the sugar hit wears off.

To keep a more even flow, it is best to select foods that release energy more slowly. These include complex carbohydrates (such as wholemeal bread, cereals and brown rice), most vegetables and fruits, and legumes (such as lentils, beans and chickpeas). If you often find yourself reaching for a cola or juice when you need an energy boost, it might be worth rethinking what you drink. Most cans of soft drink contain

9–11 teaspoons of sugar, and even fruit juice contains large amounts of sugar, without the benefits of fibre that are in the whole fruit. Healthy alternatives include water, soda water, milk, herbal teas or regular tea (not too strong). Likewise, a handful of almonds, an apple or a tub of yoghurt is a better option to get you through a long afternoon than a chocolate bar or lolly bag. Eating regular meals and frequent healthy snacks throughout the day keeps your blood sugar and energy levels more stable over time, and reduces the temptation to binge on high-glucose snacks. A decent breakfast provides fuel we need at the start of the day, so don't neglect this important meal.

Our bodies and brains require a range of vitamins and minerals to be able to function effectively. Many of these, especially Vitamin B, folate, zinc and potassium, have strong links to mood and emotions, so adequate intake is important. These can be found in many vegetables, fruits and wholegrain foods (such as oats, brown rice and rye bread).

Healthy fats (not trans fats typically found in processed biscuits, cakes and chips) also play a role in our well-being. Oily fish, eggs, nuts, avocados and dairy products are good sources of healthy fats.

Amino acids, which are found in protein, are also essential for brain and emotional health. These can be obtained by eating lean meat, fish, eggs, cheese, nuts, soya products and legumes.

As a general rule, foods and drinks that are closer to nature — that is, minimally processed and with the least amount of additives (artificial colours, flavours and preservatives) — are best for our psychological well-being. That being said, the 'yum factor' of a chocolate dessert, a packet of fries or a mega-burger are some of the little pleasures of life. They don't need to be eliminated altogether. It is more a matter of keeping it in balance, by putting these types of things on the 'occasional' list, rather than in the 'everyday' category.

ABOUT CAFFEINE

Caffeine is a stimulant drug that excites the central nervous system. It is found in coffee, tea, chocolate, colas, some medications and most energy drinks. In the short term, if you are exhausted after a long day at school and need to finish off an essay, a caffeine hit can give you a quick energy fix and increase your mental alertness. However, some people are sensitive to the effects of caffeine and even a smallish amount (one energy drink or a can of cola) can have negative effects. Caffeine can cause rapid heart rate, make you feel jittery and on-edge, and increase anxiety. If you are already in a stressed state, it can make you feel more anxious. If this is you, consider giving up caffeine and finding other ways to manage your energy. This might include regular exercise, healthy eating and giving yourself some chill-out time when your energy is low.

If you do have caffeinated drinks, consider limiting them to earlier in the day. The half-life of caffeine (that is, the length of time it takes your body to get rid of half the caffeine you have consumed) is approximately six hours. This means that if you are reaching for a late-afternoon or evening coffee 'pick-me-up', the caffeine may still be affecting you when you go to bed.

SOCIAL CONNECTION

Humans are social creatures. We are tribal by nature and hardwired to want to connect with others. We therefore enjoy having acquaintances, friends and intimate relationships. Many of us get pleasure from even brief conversations, because connecting to others is part of our make-up. For this reason, you might enjoy having a friendly chat when you stop to pat someone's dog, or when you make casual conversation at the gym.

We feel a deeper connection and sense of belonging when we are with people we know well, so spending time with friends usually gives us greater enjoyment. Friendships can be particularly satisfying, because we have things in common and we feel liked and accepted. Knowing that there are people who care about us and want to spend time with us makes us feel safe, and feeds a human instinct to belong. It can also be fun to share experiences.

Talking with others can also give us an outlet for concerns and worries, and we might benefit from getting another person's perspective. Different people may offer us different types of support. For instance, you may feel most comfortable confiding to your parents if you are feeling down, talking to a close friend about a relationship problem, turning to the school counsellor if you are experiencing school-related stress, or hopping on a moderated online forum (on a site you trust) for friendship advice.

Having some people to whom we feel connected, and to whom we can reach out for support, can play an important role in our emotional well-being. Real social connection is not a popularity contest. Striving to have the most friends will not necessarily make you feel more connected. In fact, spreading yourself too thinly can make your friendships feel superficial and unsatisfying. Instead, it is about nurturing relationships with people you can trust and depend on — it's about quality over quantity.

Building and strengthening relationships is not always simple. Some people's personalities make it easy for them to connect, because they are naturally outgoing. Others have good social support, because they have close family relationships or long-term friendships that have endured for many years. Some have been fortunate enough to come across people with whom they just 'clicked', and friendships have blossomed. If you are in any of these groups, consider yourself very lucky! For many of us, however, making friends can sometimes be a challenge. This might be because of shyness, stressful situations happening in our lives (like changing schools, depression, conflict at home, etc.) or just the lack of opportunity.

Building connections requires the courage to put yourself out there. A good place to start is by joining groups where people share a common interest (such as a sports team, debating group, chess club, choir or drama group) and meet regularly. The frequent contact enables you to get to know others over time. You might also challenge yourself to initiate conversations, even with people you don't know. This can seem hard at first, but it gets easier with time. Sometimes we need to just do it and, by so doing, learn through experience that nothing terrible happens (and even if it doesn't work out, it is rarely a disaster).

The other way to build relationships is to strengthen existing friendships. This involves making contact (via phone calls, texts, emails or social media) and initiating get-togethers. You can organise a catch-up by sending a message to say 'hi', or give them a call to let them know you are thinking of them when something big is happening in their lives.

The more of a friend and support you are to others, the more likely it is that they will be the same for you. Being a good listener and showing genuine interest in their problems also helps to build connection. Most importantly, a willingness to share some of your own self-doubts or vulnerabilities allows people to get to know the real you, and is the key to building close relationships.

BALANCE SCREEN LIFE WITH REAL LIFE

Screens, devices and social media play a huge role in our lives. They provide ways to connect with people, from friends, relatives and potential love interests, to people who live on the other side of the planet who share our passions. Technology provides avenues for staying in touch and keeping updated. In the online world, access to information about pretty much anything is at our fingertips. Opportunities for being amused and entertained are infinite. There are countless ways to share experiences, have cyber conversations, and give and receive feedback. There are also those crazy videos and funny images, which are great for a giggle when you need one.

The digital world has so much to offer that is positive but it is also easy to become consumed by it, at the expense of other important things (like sleeping and spending face-to-face time with friends). When it comes to our cyber-selves and our emotional well-being, finding a balance between our 'screen life' and our 'real life' is essential.

In a recent study, a group of teenagers were made to go tech-free for twenty-four hours — the internet, mobile phones and other screens and devices were banned. During this time, the participants' thoughts, behaviour and mood were monitored. Can you guess what happened? How do you think you would feel if you were in this position?

Teenagers involved in the project reported feeling isolated, stressed, fidgety and even panicky. The researchers described some of their symptoms as similar to those of drug addicts going into withdrawal!

How is your digital life working for you? Overall, is your screen time a mood-enhancer that adds to your enjoyment, creativity and social connection? Or does the time you spend online have a negative impact on how you feel and behave? Do you feel in control over how you use technology, or is it something that controls you?

Here are a few more questions to help you reflect on this issue:

➤ Am I spending more and more time online, and prioritising it over other important things in my life (e.g. hanging out with friends, talking with my family, playing sport, getting involved in school and community activities, working, studying or getting enough sleep)?

➤ Has the amount of time I spend on screens created negative consequences for me? (For example, marks deteriorating because I'm too distracted to focus on my work, having arguments with my parents, or pulling out of something I was looking forward to because I couldn't bring myself to 'log off'.)

➤ Have I found myself obsessing over certain sites or games to the point that I can't stop thinking about them and it is almost impossible to resist getting on them?

➤ Do I get stressed out if I can't get online, or access certain games or sites? (For example, have I not enjoyed a holiday because the Wi-Fi reception was patchy?) Am I constantly checking social media, even when I should be focusing on something else?

➤ Does spending time on certain social media sites leave me feeling down or anxious?

➤ Does screen time at night prevent me from getting into bed at a decent hour, or make it hard for me to fall asleep once I am in bed?

If you answered 'yes' to any of these questions, then reviewing your cyber use might be a good thing to do. Make sure that it is something that enhances your physical and mental health, rather than detracting from it. Here are some ways that you can keep it working for you:

➤ *Do a 'digi-audit'* to increase your self-awareness about when and how you are using technology. Keep a log of all the times that you are online, and write down how you feel during and after each online activity. Notice any positive or negative emotional reactions (such as feeling happy as you look over a friend's photos because they bring back good memories, or fuming at your parents because they are insisting you leave a multi-player game to sit down to a family dinner). Scrolling through your phone or flitting around the web is often such an automatic habit, you may not even think about it. Make 'screen time' something you do consciously — choose to use it in ways that work for you.

➤ *Plan your time online.* Set rules for yourself about how and when you are going to use technology. For example, if you are organising a dinner with friends, you might all agree in advance to ban phones at the table. If you need to get some homework finished, you might choose to block all games for a couple of hours, then reward yourself with some playing time when you are done. If you find yourself losing track of time when you're online, set an alarm to remind you when to press the 'off' button.

➤ *Keep a reality check on social media posts.* If you find yourself feeling down after looking at other people's posts and pictures, it is important to keep things in perspective. On social media, people often put up their 'highlights reel'. They display selfies taken from the most flattering angle (using the best filters) and only post updates when they are doing something exciting or cool (or seemingly so). If you are comparing yourself to these, chances are you are contrasting your 'everyday' to their 'best of', or simply getting unrealistic ideas about how good other people's lives really are. The things you read online are not a realistic basis for assessing other people's lives, or comparing them with your own. If your self-esteem is affected these types of posts, or by the number of 'likes' and comments you get on social media, it could be a good idea to re-evaluate the way you interpret this information, and how you use your time.

➤ *Balance screen time with some 'green time'.* Spending time in nature is linked to a reduction in stress, and an increase in energy and positive emotions. Exposure to sunlight encourages the brain to release serotonin, which can calm your body and lift your mood. If you are spending hours indoors looking at screens, make sure you take some breaks and head outside.

➤ *Organise real-life catch-ups.* The cyber world offers so many opportunities to meet and connect with people. Online, there are places you can develop supportive networks, get advice, share interests and just have fun with others. All of this is great, but it should not replace 'in-person' contact. Human brains are wired to respond to body language, facial expressions and tone of voice. Think about how contagious laughter can be when you are with a person who is in hysterics, or how reassuring a hug or an arm around your shoulder can be when you are going through a tough time. You cannot replace these online. Virtual interactions have much to offer, but be sure to spend quality 'real-life' time with friends and other people as well.

ATTITUDE OF GRATITUDE

Many of us get caught up focusing on what is not going well in our lives. You might find yourself dwelling on all the 'bad' in the world after watching the nightly news, or feeling jaded about relationships after an argument with a friend. While it is helpful to identify and address the challenges we face, habitually focusing on the negatives creates an unrealistic perspective and makes us feel bad. If you have a negative thinking bias, it means you are not giving equal weight to all the good things that are happening around you.

Research shows that we can boost our emotional well-being by deliberately choosing to think about what is going well in our lives — what we feel grateful for. This can be as simple as consciously making a note of the positives as we go about our day. For instance, you might recognise that you enjoyed having a conversation with another student at the bus stop today. Or that you felt a sense of achievement when you completed that long assignment. Or you might have enjoyed today's blue sky and sunshine, because you took some time to sit outside. Doing regular 'gratitude exercises' can help you develop a more balanced outlook.

Psychologist Martin Seligman has found significant mental health benefits for people who do the 'Three Good Things' exercise. This involves spending a few minutes at the end of each day reflecting on and writing down three things that went well today and the reasons why. For a 'feel-good' effect, try it for yourself.

Here are some examples of things you might include on your 'Three Good Things' list:

➤ I got my history essay in on time, because I have been working hard on it.

➤ I had a good conversation with a guy in the year above me on the bus this morning, because I wasn't wearing my headphones.

➤ I managed to get my bike fixed, because I asked my neighbour for help.

➤ I had a good talk with Dad tonight, because I was willing to tell him what was bothering me.

➤ I had a laugh with the boys at lunchtime, because we get on well and have a similar sense of humour.

➤ I did a really good workout at the gym, because I pushed myself extra hard.

➤ I enjoyed lasagne for dinner tonight, because I had told Mum it was my favourite meal and so she made it for me.

Reflect

Write down three things that went well for you today, and why they happened:

IN A NUTSHELL ...

➤ To maintain a healthy psychological state, we need to look after our physical as well as our emotional needs. Our physical needs include having a healthy diet, doing regular exercise and getting adequate sleep.

➤ In addition, nurturing good social relationships, balancing screen life with real life and developing gratitude for the good things happening in our lives also helps to protect our psychological well-being.

FIFTEEN

Support and Resources

SPEAK UP AND REACH OUT

While some of the strategies described in this book may help you through difficult times, there could be some situations where they are not enough. If you are feeling overwhelmed, highly stressed, depressed, not in control, or like you are struggling to cope, it is essential to speak up and reach out for support. Talking through your issues with someone you trust will help you feel better. A listening ear can make a real difference.

Think of three people in your life who you can turn to when you are going through a hard time (people you know can support you, e.g. your parents, a particular friend, another relative, a teacher or a school counsellor).

Support Person 1:

Support Person 2:

Support Person 3:

TELEPHONE AND ONLINE COUNSELLING

Sometimes it can be hard to reach out to someone you know (maybe they are not available, or the time just isn't right). In these cases, there are telephone and online services you can turn to. These are generally confidential (you don't have to identify yourself) and free. A number of them operate day and night, so even if it is 3 am, there is always someone available who can offer you support.

In Australia, here are some good options:

➤ **Kids Helpline**: 1800 55 1800 (phone counselling offered 24/7. For ages 5–25 years: free and confidential)
Web chat and email counselling also available at *kidshelp.com.au*

➤ **Lifeline**: 13 11 14 (phone counselling offered 24/7. For all ages: free and confidential)
Web chat also available at *lifeline.org.au*

➤ **eheadspace**: 1800 650 890 (phone counselling offered seven days a week, 9 am–1 am. For ages 12–25 years: free and confidential)
Web chat and email counselling also available at *eheadspace.org.au*

➤ **beyondblue Support Service**: 1300 22 4636 (phone counselling offered 24/7. For all ages: free and confidential)
Web chat and email counselling also available at *youthbeyondblue.com*

➤ **Suicide Call Back Service**: 1300 659 467 (phone counselling offered 24/7 if you, or anyone you know, is feeling suicidal. For all ages: free)
Web chat and video chat also available at *suicidecallbackservice.org.au*

IN-PERSON SUPPORT

Face-to-face professional counselling can also make a huge difference when you are going through a difficult time. You could start by talking to your school counsellor or GP. Your GP can refer you to a psychologist, psychiatrist or other mental-health practitioner. These people are experts and can enable you to understand what is going on for you, and help you find ways to deal with stressful situations and manage your emotions.

For more information about the different types of health professionals available and how you can access their services, take a look at the 'Types of Help' section at the ReachOut website: *au.reachout.com*.

ONLINE SUPPORT AND INFORMATION

Before you head online for mental health support and information, just remember that not everything you come across in your search will always be helpful or in your best interests. As you probably know, online there is the good, the bad and the ugly (that is, sites that are harmful and undermining). Stick to trusted sites that have an established reputation, such as those below.

SUGGESTED WEBSITES

➤ **ReachOut** (au.reachout.com): This website aims to improve mental health in young people, and is specially designed for twelve to twenty-five year olds. It contains information and advice on a wide range of topics, including managing low mood and anxiety, eating disorders, body-image issues, bullying, sexuality, friendships and relationships. There are moderated forums where you can chat to others about any challenges you are dealing with. ReachOut has regularly updated information about helpful websites and apps, and can direct you to support services in your area.

➤ **Youthbeyondblue** (youthbeyondblue.com): This website aims to help twelve to twenty-five year olds and their families and friends deal with depression and anxiety. It contains information, support and moderated forums.

➤ **Bite Back** (biteback.org.au): This website, run by the Black Dog Institute, is for twelve to eighteen year olds and aims to improve well-being and mental fitness.

FREE INTERACTIVE ONLINE SELF-HELP PROGRAMS

➤ **The Brave Program** (brave4you.psy.uq.edu.au): This program is designed to help young people manage anxiety and worries.

➤ **e-couch** (ecouch.anu.edu.au): This program contains modules that focus on managing depression, generalised anxiety and worry, social anxiety, relationship breakdown, and loss and grief. (Not specifically for teenagers.)

➤ **MoodGYM** (moodgym.anu.edu.au): This program uses CBT to help people prevent or cope with depression. (Not specifically for teenagers.)

➤ **Smiling Mind** (smilingmind.com.au): This website contains free online mindfulness meditation programs, designed to assist people in dealing with the pressure, stress and challenges of daily life.

FREE APPS

➤ **ReachOut Breathe**: This app helps you reduce the physical symptoms of stress and anxiety, by encouraging you to slow down your breathing rate (and monitoring your heart rate).

➤ **ReachOut WorryTime**: This app gives you a place to store your worries, and alerts you when it's time to think about them. When a worry no longer matters to you, you can ditch it and move on.

➤ **ReachOut Recharge**: This app focuses on improving mood, energy and well-being by putting in place good sleep/wake patterns.

➤ **Smiling Mind**: This app provides guided meditations for all age groups.

➤ **1Giant Mind**: This app also provides guided meditations for all age groups.

For up-to-date information about a range of helpful apps for teenagers, as well as reviews from people who have used them, take a look at 'The Toolbox' at: au.reachout.com/sites/thetoolbox.

FINALLY ...

We hope that you have enjoyed reading *Good Thinking*, and that it has provided some strategies that you will find useful as you make your way through life's journey. No doubt you, like all of us, will face times that are stressful, disappointing, frustrating, annoying and scary. Although life is not always smooth sailing, please know that the difficult times will pass and you will ultimately get through whatever comes your way. We hope that the ideas and tools provided in this book will make your journey a little smoother. Here's to the ups and downs, and all the in-betweens!

SARAH AND LOUISE

Index